Tramway Museum S

60th Anniversary Edition 1955-2015

Comprising the text and photographs first published in 2005 to mark the 50th Anniversary of the Tramway Museum Society

By Ian Yearsley

Plus additional material documenting the years 2005-2015

By Paul Abell and Lynn Wagstaff

With contributions from colleagues at the Museum

Revised and updated edition published by the Tramway Museum Society, National Tramway Museum, Crich, near Matlock, Derbyshire DE4 5DP

ISBN No. 978-0-949007-06-3

The ceremonial handover of Southampton 45 in which Jay Fowler, representing the LRTL, drove 45 out of Marton Depot, Blackpool, and handed the controller key to Major Charles Walker, representing the embryonic TMS, who then drove it back in again.

A R Robinson

Foreword 1955-2015

by Colin Heaton, Chairman, TMS Board of Management

The Tramway Museum Society was born out of need. It was a time of growing prosperity and optimism except, that is, for the British electric tramcar. A small collection of vehicles gathered from the late 1940s began to grow as Britain's tramways closed down. Amazingly, there were people who cared enough to attempt the unthinkable; to make their own operating Museum. On a November night in 1955 the Tramway Museum Society was born in Swan Street, Manchester. A small group gathered to set up the Tramway Museum Society dedicated to preserving what was to many an anachronistic form of transport to be thrown away without a backward glance as soon as possible.

At first the new Society did not prosper, membership was small and yet, as the imminent end of the trams became more obvious the urgency grew, and with it, the desire to find a place to preserve and demonstrate for all that fascinating form of transport little valued by many. The late 1950s were hard times for the Society and by 1959 money was still short, membership low and the few preserved trams were often in peril, indeed whole tramways had closed and the new Society had been unable to rescue anything. The dark clouds of final closure were looming over the last networks in Leeds, Sheffield, Grimsby and Immingham, Glasgow and Blackpool when the site at Crich was discovered and selected as suitable for a museum. Then fortunes changed. There was somewhere to put the precious trams. That was when the people came. The people who became the thriving Society and laboured long and hard to build their Museum. Membership grew attracting men and women from many different walks of life with one thing in common; a love of trams and a desire to save something for posterity.

Remarkably, by the mid-1960s, the members had something they had perhaps not expected and that was an operating electric tramway which had become a tourist attraction. Visitors came and paid money to see and experience what had been derided by many only years previously. The Museum grew rapidly and so did the skills of the Members. Physical strength and intellect were needed in great measure and the diversity of the membership provided both, often at great cost to individuals. Many of the people in the images are memories now, but we benefit from their foresight and labour.

As we celebrate the 60th Anniversary of the Tramway Museum Society and admire the trams, the tramway, the street scene, our exhibitions and archive and all the other things which we now have, I ask you as you read this book, to bear in mind the people, the members of the Tramway Museum Society, the staff of the Museum and those supporters who have helped but never been members. We should also remember our funders who have shown faith in our work at Crich and perhaps take modest pride in what we have.

The Society has grown over the years in two ways - its precious artefacts and its people. There could not have been the former without the latter and the contributions of many hundreds of people through the 60 years we are commemorating in this volume form a huge part of the Society's history. The Tramway Museum Society still depends on workers, supporters and visitors for its work to prosper.

I commend this history of our Society's work to all who read it and thank the people whose story it is, for their skills and vision. I also thank the compilers of this new volume for their combined work in its production.

Tramway Museum Story 1955-2005

by Ian Yearsley

The first General Meeting of the Tramway Museum Society was held at the Bakers' Institute, 56 Swan Street, Manchester at 7 p.m. on 18th November 1955. Sixteen members and two press representatives were present.

In the absence of the (prospective) Chairman of the Society, Major C S N Walker, the chair was taken by Mr R B Parr, who read the following address from Major Walker.

"I am very sorry I cannot be with you for your opening meeting, but I find that the pressure of my work and other duties make this impossible. I hope, however, that despite my absence the Society will get off to a good start.

"The tram in this country is in a peculiar position; not quite ancient enough to be called an antique and so earning place in a museum, but unfortunately so rapidly disappearing from our streets that a generation is growing up who have never known them, let alone ride in them. It behoves us, therefore, to preserve what we have got for posterity. At a later date we may get support from official sources, but we must not count on this, as this country is not as transport minded as are some continental countries. Till then we have a duty to perform.

"Tram cars are very bulky and are therefore costly to move and store, so it is essential to make every endeavour to attract as many subscribers as we possibly can, for until we have some money we cannot show the cars as they should be shown, and until they are shown we cannot expect much, if any, support from the outside public.

"Much hard work has already been done, but more still remains to be done. You will hear what the Museum Committee has done so far and most grateful thanks are extended to those who have put in so much time and work, and to those who have been so patient over outstanding debts. Let us now try all we can to increase this faithful band so that the cars we have may once again be shown as they were in their heyday."

It was resolved to thank Major Walker for his message.

Mr J H Price read a full report on tramway museum activities by the LRTL during the past seven years, commencing with the acquisition of Southampton No. 45 in 1948 and the formation of a Museum Committee in 1949.

Mr Price pointed out that with the exception of Southampton No. 45, the acquisition of which was fully covered by donations, each car had been financed mostly by loans from individual members of the LRTL Museum Committee, who had been partly repaid from donations received.

The vehicles owned are Southampton open-top car No. 45, Newcastle bogie car No. 102, Cardiff water car No. 131, Douglas Head Marine Drive open-top car No. 1, Leeds No. 446 totally-enclosed ex-Hull car, Liverpool single deck trailer car No. 129, the remains of Liverpool Bellamy car No. 558, a Peckham Cantilever truck, a Brill 21E swing-link truck, towing lorry EN4501 and two road trailers.

Extract from TMS Newsletter No. 8, November 1958.

This book commemorates fifty years of the Tramway Museum Society (TMS). It does so at a time when the TMS has much to celebrate. A fleet of more than 50 trams, more than 90 per cent of them presentably restored, and more than 80 per cent having operated at some time on its own tracks, is housed under cover. At its National Tramway Museum (NTM) at Crich, Derbyshire, more than 40 per cent. of the fleet is currently on the operating roster; they can be seen in a mature yet still developing street scene, while on busiest days as many as 15 cars will run, carrying visitors on a mile-long track, laid entirely with grooved tramway rail.

At the NTM, visitors will find a workshop which turns out restorations of outstanding quality, a library which attracts researchers from all over the world, a well-stocked bookshop, tea-rooms and a rebuilt pub, the Red Lion. There is a Tramways Trade Exhibition of 1905, vividly recreated, a viewing gallery for the workshop, two special areas for children, and a widely-acclaimed woodland walk. All this in a museum which is still independent, run by the TMS whose 2,500 members come from all walks of life and many parts of the world. It is museum without any burden of debt which has won awards for excellence and has national Designation and a royal patron.

The TMS also faces ongoing challenges. Once the only attraction of its kind, its museum now faces competition not only from commercial theme parks, subsidised museums and heritage sites, but also from Sunday shopping. From a peak of 204,000 in 1978, visitor numbers slowly declined to less than half that number, but determined marketing efforts in recent years have now begun to reverse that trend. And the spend per visitor has been increasing. Much effort in the coming years will have to be made simply to ensure that the Museum remains a popular day-out destination for families: one to which they want to return and bring others.

There are also challenges because trams are still being offered for preservation, and if accepted, accommodation has to be found for them, as well as eventual funding for restoration.

So how did all this come about? The Tramway Museum Society dates from 1955, and has its origins in the Museum Committee of the Light Railway Transport League (LRTL) (now the Light Rail Transit Association), of which more later. There are really two starting dates in 1955. The LRTL held a Convention at Blackpool in May, and at Blackpool's Marton Depot, hidden away among the Corporation's own cars, was Southampton 45, an open top car preserved by the LRTL in 1948. Already the idea of a separate Tramway Museum Society had been taking shape, and a ceremony was arranged in which Jay Fowler, representing the LRTL, drove 45 out of Marton Depot and handed the controller key to Major Charles Walker, representing the embryonic TMS, who then drove it back in again.

This ceremony is always seen as the start of the TMS but it actually predated the formation of the Society by six months. Not until Friday 18 November 1955 was the inaugural TMS meeting held, in a small room at the Bakers' Institute, Swan Street, Manchester. Sixteen people were present, plus two press representatives, and the constitution it then adopted made it clear that the objective was to establish and maintain a working tramway museum.

At the meeting in Manchester Bob Parr took the chair in the absence of Charles Walker, whose appointment as chairman of the Society was confirmed. Other appointments were John Price as honorary secretary; Ralph Jackson, honorary treasurer; Geoff Hyde, honorary assistant treasurer; and as ordinary committee members Norman Forbes, George Hearse, Bob Parr, Keith Pearson, Cliff Taylor and Richard Wiseman. Shortly afterwards, Richard Wiseman became honorary assistant secretary. Others known to have been present were Jack Batty, W Gwynne Thomas, Basil Miller, Terence Goulding, Alan Ralphs and Dennis Gill.

From the LRTL they took over assets comprising Southampton 45, Newcastle 102, Cardiff 131, Douglas Southern 1, Leeds 446 (Hull 132), Liverpool 429, the dismantled Liverpool

Bellamy 558, a Peckham cantilever truck, a Brill 21E swing-link truck, towing lorry EN4501 and two road trailers.

The last three items represented an attempt by the LRTL Museum Committee to carry out its own tramcar moves to save haulage costs. The former Bury Transport breakdown truck EN4501 had been rebuilt from a pre-war Leyland Titan bus and latterly carried the TMS title on its front. One of the trailers was a closed van; the other, an ex-fairground trailer on solid tyres, was used to move the Peckham cantilever truck from Leeds to Wike's Mill, Bury, but adventures with overheated bearings en route discouraged further moves with this vehicle.

But at this point I need to explain more about the LRTL Museum Committee, both what it achieved and why it had to give way to a separate Tramway Museum Society. The story begins in Southampton in 1948. Since its formation in 1937, the LRTL had been trying to stem the tide of decline in tramways in Britain, campaigning under slogans such as "modernise and develop the tramways" and in the process it brought together enthusiasts who studied detail and history as well as determined campaigners. One of its activities was to run tours by special car on tramway systems throughout the country, for the 1930s torrent of tramway abandonments, halted by the war, was now starting up again slowed only by delays in delivery of new buses.

Between a standard and a Vambac car, Southampton 45, then owned by the LRTL, takes the air outside Blackpool's Marton Depot.

National Tramway Museum

One such tour took place in Southampton on Sunday, 29 August 1948. With its mixture of modern-looking domed-roofed vehicles and open-top knifeboard cars, Southampton was popular with enthusiasts, and LRTL members from Birmingham, Manchester and Glasgow joined others from London and the southern counties to take part.

It was in effect to be a farewell; though several routes were still running, buses had been ordered. At the start of 1948 the system had been intact save for the Northam route which had closed in 1936. But the last cars ran to Bitterne Park on 15 May 1948 and open-top cars had scarcely been seen in service since Whit. Monday. So on 29 August, domed-roof car 37, one of those repainted in post-war cherry red livery, began the tour, running first to Floating Bridge, and after a delay at Docks station to fix a detached trolleyhead, it took the party first to Millbrook and then to Portswood depot where rows of open-top cars, still in wartime grey paint, were stored out of service.

As it was a fine day, a change to one of these was requested. Such a request might have foundered on bureaucracy in many larger tramway systems, but Southampton was flexible and accommodating, and so knifeboard open-top car 44 was brought out to continue the tour. The only open car out on that warm day, it ran via Swaythling and Bassett out to Shirley Depot, back to Royal Pier, and then to a restaurant in the city centre for tea. It waited while members took a ferry trip to Hythe and back, and finally took the party back to the Central Station. Asking what would become of 44 after this, they were told that its next journey would be to the scrapyard.

Newcastle 102 at the Montagu Motor Museum, Beaulieu, after Southampton 45 had been moved to Crich and its place at Beaulieu was filled by a Portsmouth trolleybus.

Mike Crabtree

This hit hard, and on the train back to London the idea of purchasing one of these cars was born. Enquiry was made, and Southampton general manager Percy Baker offered one for £10. More than that, he chose the car with the best body condition, 45, united it with newly-tyred wheelsets from another car, and put the result through the works as a routine overhaul. And so 45 emerged in what would have been the post-war colours of cherry red and cream, had these cars ever been repainted from wartime camouflage grey.

Though the purchase price was a nominal and generous £10, some £40 had to be raised for the car's removal. An appeal was launched in October 1948 among LRTL members nationally, who raised £66/3/8d in donations ranging from 2s 6d (12½p) to £1, mostly paid by postal orders. News of the appeal quickly reached local LRTL regions, and at a Manchester meeting I gave half-a-crown (2s 6d), thus unwittingly assuring myself of a place at the 50-year celebrations of tramcar preservation in 1998. A small investment, but what a return on it!

All this may have seemed like a foolhardy venture on the part of the LRTL members. But from the United States they already had several examples of what amateurs could do, not merely to preserve, but to operate trams. Branford Electric Railway Association, launched in 1945, had taken over an operating line in 1947 and continued to run it, and a brief but telling description of this was published in the LRTL's journal 'Modern Tramway' in November 1948. Two other American trolley museums, Seashore Electric Railway at Kennebunkport and the Connecticut Electric Railway Museum at Warehouse Point, were formed respectively in 1939 and 1948, though they did not start operating cars until 1953 and 1954. Nevertheless, just as in the early days of electric tramways when much of the technology came from across the Atlantic, much of the inspiration for a concerted programme of tramway preservation in this country came in 1948 from America.

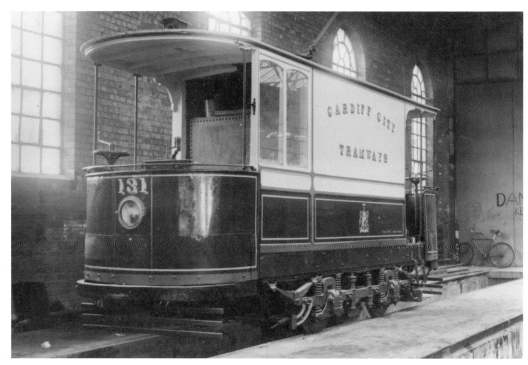

Cardiff water car 131 was missed off the scrap dealer's list and so became available for preservation. On 8 May 1959 it was the first to arrive at the Tramway Museum Society's newly-acquired site at Crich.

I L Wright

At its Blackpool Convention in May 1949, the LRTL set up a separate Museum Committee, though to avoid conflicts with its campaigning work, museum activities were not publicised in 'Modern Tramway' for some considerable time. The LRTL members were able to view their purchase, by then safely stored in Marton Depot where 45 was to remain until 1958. It had come by a circuitous route: delivered at first to Kirkstall Road Works, Leeds, under a verbal but unconfirmed agreement, it was brought to Blackpool by Baker's, the Southampton haulage contractors, who were delivering domed-roof cars and trucks to Leeds at that time.

With the Branford example before them, the new Museum Committee from the start had the vision of a working tramway museum, run by an enthusiast body. The scrapping in 1948 of two Manchester cars, balcony 686 and single-deck 847 after ten years' semi-preservation in the works fleet, convinced them that operators on their own could not be relied upon to preserve trams. Brighton 55 and Lytham 43 were among other operator-preserved cars which had been scrapped, though efforts by an individual enthusiast, Dr H A Whitcombe, had put the 1867 Ryde Pier car and a Portstewart steam tram engine into the Hull Transport Museum and Reece Winstone had parts of a London Street Tramways horse car in store.

It should be noted that this predated the start of the railway preservation movement in this country; the Talyllyn Railway Preservation Society (TRPS), which began that movement, was created only in 1951. But the supporters of the Museum Committee were few in number, and its first car, 45, was the only one which came debt-free. Most subsequent cars were paid for by loans from individual members acting as sponsors. Repayment of these loans, as well as finding secure lodging for tramcars, remained a prime concern of the committee and, from 1955, of the TMS, right up to 1959 when the Crich site became available.

The Museum Committee's second car, Newcastle 102, was accepted in May 1950, two months after the city ceased to run its own trams. It was at first stored in Newcastle's Byker Depot, but was then moved, first to Hodgson's Garage, Benton, and then in 1954 to Bury, where it stood on tracks in the former tram depot until 1958 when it had to be removed in the face of the Town Clerk's ultimatum. A project to buy a Cardiff low-height car fell through because all had been sold to a scrap dealer, but it was then found that a water car, 131, had been omitted from the scrap deal, and this was acquired and moved to Allensbank Works, Cardiff.

In November 1960 Sheffield 510, Southampton 45, Sheffield 189 and Sheffield 46 occupy some of the first standard gauge track to be laid at Crich. Earlier that month, the three Sheffield cars had been in the city's tramway farewell procession

National Tramway Museum / R B Parr

Leeds 446, the last of a batch of cars obtained from Hull, joined the fleet, and the body was moved to War Department property at Atherton, for restoration as Hull 132. Before it left Leeds, however, it was used for a tour of the City's tramways and a 'Yorkshire Post' report of this on 22 October 1951 further strained relations between the Museum Committee and the parent LRTL by stressing the nostalgia aspects of tramway enthusiasm such as collecting photographs and destination blinds.

'Modern Tramway' in December 1951 reported that Museum Committee activities would in future appear in 'Tramway Review', the LRTL's newly-established historical magazine, and it was here early in 1952 that John Price set out at some length the need for a tramway museum. He rightly predicted that a separate body would have to be set up on the lines of the Talyllyn Railway Preservation Society (TRPS), which had then been in existence for a year. He believed that historic cars should not be left scattered to rust in depots but should be brought together in a museum with a demonstration track where visitors could ride on them. But at that time he also thought that the expense of setting up a permanent tramway museum would be beyond the capacity of tramway enthusiasts alone, and help would be needed from the public transport industry.

Southampton 45 on the newly-laid southbound track at the Museum, showing the destination Crich Town End; the practice of displaying such destinations was soon dropped in favour of home-town indications

Ian Yearsley

With £80 still owing in repayment of loans, and publicity still restricted because of the need to avoid conflict with the LRTL's main campaign, this view was understandable. Indeed at that time the Museum Committee was unable to raise funds even to provide sheeting for two Liverpool cars, Bellamy 558 and single-deck trailer 429. These were stored in the open at Kirkby, subject to weather and vandalism damage, and eventually they had to be disposed of as scrap in December 1954 and early 1955.

Vandalism also affected the Scottish Tramway Museum Society (STMS), now the Scottish Tramway and Transport Society, formed in 1953 initially to save Paisley 68, then still running as 1068 in the Glasgow fleet. Glasgow Corporation agreed to store it, first in Elderslie Depot and from 1957 was at Dalmarnock, where it survived in safety. But the STMS had less fortune with Aberdeen's last balcony car, 73. Privately sponsored, it was moved by the STMS to storage in Paisley, getting jammed under a bridge on the way, but then suffered vandalism damage so extensive that it had to be scrapped. Several Dublin cars, stored in the open air near the Sutton terminus of the Hill of Howth tramway in Ireland, suffered similar damage in the early 1950s. Vandalism was an ever-present fear for trams stored in urban areas, particularly on open-air sites, and was one of the factors that led the search to rural areas for a museum site.

Bowmer & Kirkland's crane is assembled ready to transfer newly-arrived Blackpool 167 on to its bogies on some of the newly-laid standard gauge tram track.

Ian Yearsley

Despite all its own problems, the LRTL Museum Committee had had success as a catalyst for other preservation projects. Douglas Southern Electric Tramways car 1 of 1896, saved by enthusiasts from the Marine Drive's Little Ness Depot, was offered to the then British Transport Commission (BTC) for its Museum of British Transport at Clapham and accepted in 1956. Later on, the newly-created TMS played a similar role with Llandudno 6, ex-Bournemouth 85, for which Alfred Richardson of Rhyl met the purchase cost, the TMS provided funds for its move, and BTC received and housed it at Clapham.

This however followed in the wake of a project which could have changed the whole course of preservation in this country. The Llandudno & Colwyn Bay Electric Railway (L&CBER) was the last remaining company-owned tramway in the country (the Swansea & Mumbles line, owned by South Wales Transport, was legally a railway). The L&CBER ran a mixture of single-deck and mostly open-top double-deck cars over a 6½ mile 3ft. 6in. gauge line through a remarkable variety of scenery in a holiday area, but early in 1955 plans for its closure were announced.

Hard to imagine that Manchester 765, seen here at Crich in 1961, would be fully restored and able to run at the Museum in 1977-78, before moving to Heaton Park. It has also run at Blackpool

Ian Yearsley

In March 1955, a leaflet was enclosed with 'Modern Tramway' from a body called the Tramway Preservation Committee, announcing that it had an option to purchase the L&CBER. The story of its negotiations is set out in some detail by Geoff Price in his book 'Llandudno & Colwyn Bay Trams since 1945' and it appeared that the original asking price of £7,500 was progressively raised to a figure about four times that amount, and so the project failed. Though not named in the leaflet, the committee is understood to have comprised Lionel Boylett, Richard Elliott, Jay Fowler, H G Huntley, Claude Lane and Edward Piercy. Had it succeeded, the whole story of tramway preservation would have been different and it is likely that neither the museum at Crich nor the tramway at Seaton would have come to fruition. Instead, the accent would have been on operating a narrow gauge seaside tramway and enthusiasts would have found themselves driving trams in real traffic on the streets of Llandudno, Rhos-on-Sea and Colwyn Bay.

The skeleton of Manchester 765 stands alongside the future main line in front of Leicester 99 which was serving as a tea hut, on 4 March 1961.

Ian Yearsley

Jay Fowler was also the prime mover in the preservation of Sunderland 100, otherwise Metropolitan Electric Tramways centre-entrance Feltham car 331. With Sunderland tramways due to close in 1954, an appeal to save this car was launched in February 1953, and it was stored in Bishop Auckland until 1957 when it was moved to Bradford's Thornbury Works. This car may well have been the inspiration for the original badge of the LRTL, of which organisation Jay Fowler was chairman.

Many preservation projects failed, however. Stockport 55 was chosen, replaced by 101, but there was nowhere to keep it. Schemes for a Leeds pivotal car and Manchester 106 (Aberdeen 49) came to nothing. Blackpool general manager Walter Luff offered toastrack 163 in 1955. The work of Dr H A Whitcombe has already been mentioned. And in 1947, Gwynne Thomas, then still a schoolboy, attempted to buy a Bolton balcony car!

By the mid-1950s, the LRTL was having to campaign strongly even in those cities where the tramcar's future had seemed secure and where new cars had even been bought in the post-war years. Aberdeen, Glasgow, Edinburgh, Leeds and Sheffield were all making moves towards tramway replacement. Given the conflict of aims with the Museum Committee, it was time to float a separate society, and so came the events of 1955, the ceremonial handover of Southampton 45 on 29 May, and the inaugural meeting on 18 November.

John Markham and Jack Batty working on the overhead wiring at Town End in 1964, shortly before the first trolley wire was installed.
Mike Crabtree

David Rennard hands over the outdoor tramcar maintenance pit to Tony Bacon after 330 has demonstrated that the bearers across the former powder magazine will bear the weight.
Mike Crabtree

Even before the TMS was formed, the LRTL Museum Committee had been searching for a museum site, and places visited included various Pennine quarries in 1952, Bacup locomotive shed in 1954, and the TMS looked at Cedric Road, a site near Heaton Park, Manchester in 1956. A goods shed at Baxenden, the site of the former Easingwold Railway near York, former tram depots at Horwich and Pyewipe, Grimsby, were all examined. There was also Webb's Tannery siding at Hertford, a farm near Burghclere, Merstham Quarry near Reigate, a railway site at Selhurst and a brickworks at Ascot. Talks were held with Blackpool about possible storage of cars at Copse Road, Fleetwood, but no progress was made. As notices to quit began to appear on tramcar storage sites, the search grew ever more urgent.

By the time of its second annual meeting in Manchester on 1 December 1956, the TMS had 65 members, and membership remained at about this number until the move to the Crich site in 1959. Attempts by the TMS and the STMS to persuade Dundee to keep a car had failed. With so many notices to quit, the options at this time for several cars seemed *Extract from TMS Newsletter No. 8, November 1958.*

Montagu Motor Museum - Work Report, June to October 1958

Work has continued throughout the summer on the lines set out in previous circulars, and Southampton 45's track is now laid and ballasted. This track has been laid provisionally with one rail facing inwards, as the rails were delivered thus, and to lift and turn a 36 ft. tram rail is more than two people can manage. The next two tasks are constructing Newcastle 102's track and repainting 102's exterior. The work is far behind schedule, and unless other members attend regularly this winter it will be necessary to pay for professional assistance in repainting No. 102 by the required date of Easter, 1959, when the Museum extensions will be formally opened with considerable ceremony and publicity. Compared with American progress, the Society's inability to lay 72 ft. of track in eight months is disappointing in the extreme, and bodes ill for the chances of any larger museum scheme in this country. Moreover, lack of regular attention is bound to result in rapid deterioration in the condition of the two cars on display.

Working parties will continue as before, i.e. every fine Sunday afternoon, though members may turn up at any time and get on with digging 102's track pit or removing the old exterior paint and applying undercoat. If the weather is wet, there are small components to be painted inside No. 102, access to which is by a combination lock with the combination '9218'. All further information may be obtained from Mr N D G Mackenzie, 34 Suttry Road, Bournemouth, Hants. Mr Sedgwick has succeeded by Mr Beatty as curator of the Museum.

Expenditure to date at Beaulieu (other than the initial £330 for moving the two cars from Lancashire) is as follows:

Purchase and transport of sleepers	£36/ 10/ 0
Transport of rails and standards	14/ 6/ 9
Purchase of rail spikes	2/ 16/ 7
Transport of jacks and tracking	5/ 0/ 0
New trolley rope for car No. 102	0/ 18/ 3
Tools and sundries	4/ 4/ 2
Labour charges (up to 10th Sept.)	4/ 18/ 6
	£68/ 14/ 3

Expenditure is likely to continue at this rate for another twelve months, as it will cost about £25 to move car No. 102 on her track by crane, and about £40 to purchase and install sheeting for the top decks. The expenses to date have absorbed almost the whole of the Society's income for the year 1957/58, and no further progress is possible until the Society's funds have been replenished by next year's subscriptions; the usual subscription form is attached to this newsletter.

to be finding another museum to accept them, or disposing of them as scrap. One ray of hope in this bleak situation came from a meeting on 10 November 1957 with Lord Montagu, when he agreed to take one car, preferably 45, on permanent loan at the Montagu Motor Museum at Beaulieu, Hants. By early 1958 this had developed into a scheme for two cars, 45 and 102, to go on outdoor display there, flanking the entrance of the new museum building.

They were to stand on ex-Portsmouth tramway rail and ex-Portsdown and Horndean bracket arm poles were to be erected. "Planning restrictions would seem to prevent the acceptance of top-covered double deck tramcars," reported TMS Newsletter No. 6 in March 1958. At this time the newsletter served both to give news and to provide a record of meetings; no separate minutes were kept.

The first car to move to Beaulieu was 102 which left Bury on 19 March and arrived two days later. Southampton 45 followed on 1/2 April, and TMS working parties began to reassemble the top deck fittings of the cars and to prepare their tracks. 102 was eventually moved laterally on to its new tracks by a Royal Engineers' working party from Longmoor on 7 and 8 March 1959, and a canvas roof cover was provided on the top deck of 45. This cover, which overlapped the sides and ends to throw rainwater clear of the body, saved much damage being done to the body during its years outdoors. Shortage of funds meant that 102 was not so fortunate.

Working parties at Beaulieu sometimes consisted of one member travelling by train from London or Bournemouth to Brockenhurst. Near the station John Price had arranged for a bicycle to be kept in a garden shed; this provided transport through the New Forest to Beaulieu and back for the volunteer.

At this time a lot of interest was being taken in British and Irish tramcars by trolley museums in America, and cars from Blackpool, Liverpool, Leeds and the Hill of Howth were eventually shipped across the Atlantic. The TMS gave advice and publicity to these projects, and in December 1958, aware of the accommodation problems for cars here, the City of Portland Transport Museum made an offer for Cardiff 131, but this one was declined as by then the Crich site was in view. Sheffield Transport Committee had agreed in February 1958 to present a 1927-type car to the TMS, and to store it for up to three years in their own depots. Originally this was to have been car 195, but this was replaced later by 189 which was in better condition.

Enormous encouragement came from the restoration of Bradford balcony car 104 and its operation on a short track at Thornbury Depot for the first time on 21 July 1958. Restoration of this car, which had been used since 1950 as a scorer's box at Odsal Stadium, was made possible by the Bradford general manager, Chaceley Humpidge, who was formally installed as the first president of the TMS on 21 June 1958. At that time there was no limit on the term of office, and he remained president, fulfilling the office with distinction until his death in 1972.

One incidental result of the 104 restoration was that it revived the column for four foot gauge tramways in the Ministry of Transport annual statistics. Two years later John Price attempted to make similar statistical history; during 45's move from Beaulieu to Crich it was stopped for a traffic census on the M1 and he insisted on a special category being created for tramcars using motorways.

The Bradford revival came as a bright spot amid a series of tramway closures taking place in those years. Liverpool's last tram ran in 1957, Aberdeen's in 1958, Hill of Howth and Leeds in 1959, Swansea & Mumbles and Sheffield in 1960, Grimsby & Immingham in 1961 and Glasgow in 1962. Blackpool closed its inland routes and reduced its tram fleet in 1961-63. All these dates were critical for tramcar preservation because they imposed urgent deadlines to remove cars or see them scrapped; had for instance Aberdeen's cars run for just a year longer, one might have been preserved.

John Baggs working on the overhead wiring in 1964, the first year of electric operation at the Museum.
Mike Crabtree

Early in 1959, the whole picture changed. High in the Derbyshire hills above Matlock, Cliff Quarry, Crich, had become uneconomic to work by traditional methods and its owners, the Clay Cross Company, closed it in 1957. This made its metre-gauge railway to the lime kilns at Ambergate redundant, and the TRPS acquired quantities of its rail for shipment to Towyn (now Tywyn). Among the TRPS volunteers involved in lifting the rail in Autumn 1958 was Michael Davis, and he drew Richard Wiseman's attention to the quarry's potential as a tramway museum site.

The site was itself historic: the railway had been built by George Stephenson in 1841 to enable limestone, quarried at Crich, to be carried to the Ambergate lime-kilns, which were fired by coal from Stephenson's mines. The metre gauge chosen was probably the world's first. At the NTM the stone building, now incorporating the bookshop, was the original George Stephenson quarry forge and workshop.

The second trolleywire goes up to link with the first trolley reverser, then on the east side. Steam locomotive John Bull, minus roof, can be seen beyond Grimsby & Immingham 20, later to be disclosed as Gateshead 5
Ian Yearsley

Derwent View, a scene of mud and rubble; in the foreground, the Quarry powder magazine whose foundations served as the first inspection pit.
Ian Yearsley

The TMS Committee inspected the site on 31 January 1959, travelling its length in a quarry wagon hauled by diesel locomotive Ted on part of the remaining quarry tracks. As a result, an Extraordinary General Meeting was called on 11 April 1959 at Lilybank Hydro, Chesterfield Road, Matlock "to seek approval of a site for a tramway museum which has been found at Crich in Derbyshire through the efforts of Mr R J S Wiseman and Mr J M Davies (sic)".

Merlyn Bacon, who became honorary site manager in October 1959, described the site as it then was;

"As one entered through the present entrance there was, on the right, a deep cutting which was the roadbed of the main line of the light railway. To the left was a pile of scrap metal including the bodies of two tipping lorries. In front and slightly to the left was the engine shed which was extended forward by having a very rough timber construction built on the front. The doors were falling off! Inside the shed was Ted, the remaining light railway diesel locomotive. A narrow gauge line led from the engine shed to a headshunt alongside the cutting and the rail layout on the site and in the quarry was virtually complete. Just beyond the engine shed was the smithy, which contained two smiths' hearths and an immense amount of scrap, and this was followed by the then workshop, which at that time had two floors and a very low entrance from which a narrow gauge line led via a derelict engine shed, without a roof, to the main line of the light railway. This latter building was provided with a pit.... This then was the site as it existed except for the large piles of scrap which were everywhere and the fact that there was not a complete window in any of the buildings."

Working parties began to arrive from Birmingham, Manchester, London, Leeds, Derby, Bristol and other places. Merlyn Bacon began to weld together a crowd of enthusiasts with differing skills and abilities into a disciplined working team. Among their first tasks were to lay the foundations of the present Town End terminus by filling in the cutting up to the former bridge carrying the main road over the light railway with rubble and stones from the quarry, moved by narrow gauge train, and to clear the site of rubbish and scrap.

A word should be said here about our neighbours. Gladys Poplar, who occupied the former quarry foreman's house (now Poplar House), took a keen interest in site activities from the start. Joan Harrison and her family, whose shop then included a cafe with a 'Teas with Hovis' sign, made members feel immediately welcome, as did George Briddon and his successors at the Cliff Inn. Two local characters should also be mentioned: Wilf Harper, called "Pibber" in the village, was known to the members on the site as "Slypers" from his pronunciation of the word sleepers. He used to walk around the site each day after he finished his work at the farm by Crich Cross. There was also a recluse called "Pummy" Thompson who lived in a shack in the quarry and was occasionally seen, with his three-legged dog, on the museum site.

First steps at Crich

The committee of the TMS made its first inspection of the quarry site at Crich on Saturday, 31 January 1959, and met afterwards at the Lilybank Hydro, Chesterfield Road, Matlock, where the decision to go ahead with the Crich project was approved. It was then adopted by an Extraordinary General Meeting on 11 April. A memorandum dated 19 January from Geoffrey Claydon, the TMS hon. secretary, set out the likely costs involved in the project.

"The following are suggested as our targets:-

Year 1959 - £1,500

To cover:		
	1. Years rent	£50
	2. Reserve for rent and rates in 1960	£50
	3. Hire of vehicles in connection with levelling	£50
	4. Alterations to buildings, etc.	£100
	5. Track	£100
	6. Purchase of overhead equipment	£50
	7. Transport of track, poles, etc.	£50
	8. New building fund	£750
	9. Transport of cars to Crich	£300
		£1,500

Year 1960 - £1,000

To cover:		
	1. Rent and rates reserves	£100
	2. Purchase of Leeds and Liverpool cars	£250
	3. Transport of cars	£400
	4. Further purchases of track and overhead material	£150
	5. New building fund	£100
		£1,000

After 1960 it should be possible to manage on subscription income plus possible appeals for the purchase of rectifying equipment, track, etc."

In a note he suggested that Sheffield would be a source of poles and brackets, and "Leeds members might like to remove the poles in Middleton Woods."

In his covering letter, Geoffrey Claydon noted that "in the event of inclement weather, it is desirable to wear footwear adequate to withstand mud or deep snow." A decision on whether to go ahead with the project was "somewhat urgently required" as it was known that other persons were interested in acquiring the place. The premises were available at an annual rental of £50 for three years with an option to renew.

Preliminary work required included filling with rubble from the quarry of the cutting adjacent to the buildings, removal of the floor from the stone building, and levelling of the site for a new four-car shed to be built during 1960.

Very soon in 1959 cars began to arrive. Cardiff 131 was the first, on 8 May, and it was followed by Leeds 399 on 15 August and Sheffield 15, Leeds 180 and 345. Leeds 180 arrived on 6 February 1960 still numbered 189, as in its latter days in service; the old number was quickly restored. There was no standard gauge track for these first arrivals to stand on because the Talyllyn volunteers had left the quarry track in the site itself. Indeed it was not until 3 August 1959 that the first few yards of standard gauge track could be laid. And then the problem was that as fast as track was laid, more cars arrived to occupy it, for there was as yet scarcely any depot accommodation.

Sheffield 510 southbound on the single track in August 1964. On the left is Leicester 99, the mess-room and the ash filling shows the limit of the earlier horse tram operation.

Mike Crabtree

The 11 April 1959 meeting had approved a three-year lease being taken on the "bottom site" at an annual rent of £50; this excluded the powder magazine which stood at the present approach to track 10 in depot IV. The Clay Cross Company, formed originally by George Stephenson to acquire and exploit minerals at Crich and elsewhere in Derbyshire, reserved a right of way up the line, which they never exercised. By December 1960, the TMS had acquired the freehold of the same limited area for £1,000. The winter of 1959-60 saw the first new building go up, a Guildcrete agricultural barn which became known as Depot A. It fitted snugly around four cars and was erected with Howth 10 already inside; the right hand track was laid with an extra rail to Irish 5 ft. 3 in. gauge to accommodate this car. In early days there was a scheme for a separate short line to Irish gauge, and this idea surfaced again in the 1967 Development Report, though 10 has since been regauged.

If trams had been slow to come in 1959, in 1960 they came in a flood. A total of 15 cars

The first trolleywire was erected on Whit Sunday, 17 May 1964. From that date generator car 01 normally stood at the limit of the track at Quarry Approach. When generating, this car would feed power into the overhead via its trolley pole.

Jonathan Johansson Collection

arrived, four of them on one weekend. All arrived on low-loader lorries, and most were unloaded by cranes hired from Bowmer & Kirkland. But it was not to be until April 1961 that the first Atcost prefabricated building was erected, part of the present Depot II, and meanwhile rows of cars stood around, looking rather forlorn beneath tarpaulin sheets. The Atcost building, again designed for agricultural use, was chosen partly because it could accommodate three tracks with room to move around the cars. This first section held six cars, and temporary track was assembled from quarry rails to move the cars into the depot. A series of derailments on this provided much experience in jacking, packing and slewing.

Until the Sheffield permanent way crane arrived on 24 May 1962, facilities were primitive, so cars were moved by muscle-power and crowbars under the wheels. Lengths of tram rail were shifted by gangs of twenty men taking hold of the railhead and lifting, a few inches at a time, to Merlyn's instructions. Derailed trams were re-railed with jacks and wood packing. In those early years we acquired a great many skills, from installing fishplates to carrying concrete sleepers on crowbars, and today Health and Safety rules would forbid some and require a certificate for the rest. Wet weather, and the continued arrival of trams and heavy equipment, had reduced the site to a quagmire early in 1961. Only two cars arrived that year, and the first, northbound, track of what is now the main line was laid, using grooved rail from various sources on concrete sleepers.

Before the opening of workshop facilities, early restoration efforts took place in primitive conditions; Leicester 76 receives preparatory work in the open air in 1965.
Mike Crabtree

In the early days the site had no mains drainage, no gas, no electricity and no telephone. There was but one cold water tap. Members staying overnight had to sleep in trams and would discuss the relative merits of 600, 331 and 40 for this purpose. But now some amenities began to appear. The lower deck of Leicester 99, bought to provide spares for 76, was placed alongside the main line and served as a messroom. A chemical w.c. was installed at the back of the former weighbridge house. Atcost erected extensions to the main depot and late in 1962 work began on a track fan. Already a connection known as 'Bacon's curve' had been laid to give access to the stone workshop, in which the intermediate floor was removed and the door lintel raised to allow entry for a double deck car. A publication called 'Trams' (originally planned with the title 'Our Trams') was launched in 1961 and continued with 32 issues until 1969. It was designed to tell visitors and others about the TMS fleet and other activities, but it was finally superseded by the museum guide, first issued in summer 1962. From January 1961 the TMS Newsletter had been replaced by an illustrated Journal; tramcar moves on site were news and early issues included diagrams to show where cars were then standing. A bookstall was improvised, first in the entrance meter house and later in W21, an ex-Glasgow works car, positioned near the present gift shop.

Blackpool cars 40, in green, and 49, in red, at Town End, 1964. On the left are the Beauchief, Sheffield, shelter and the tea caravan.

Mike Crabtree

Meanwhile cars from the original collection had arrived at Crich. Car 45, which began the preservation story as well as that of the TMS, had wandered from Southampton to Leeds, on to Blackpool and back to Hampshire at the Montagu Motor Museum, Beaulieu, before reaching Crich on 29 October 1960. Extracting it from Beaulieu was a difficult task, made all but impossible by heavy rain; the low-loader became bogged down and the damage to lawns, flower beds, paths and drains landed the TMS with a bill for £133/5/0d. Before the Crich site was found, frequent movements of cars from one temporary home to another gave rise to waste of cash and effort as well as subjecting cars to accumulating damage.

Douglas Head Marine Drive 1 makes a rare run for members, under its own power; this view is from the 'blind' side, originally away from the road and against the cliff.

Mike Crabtree

Most cars arriving at Crich were sponsored by local groups and were in conditions varying from ready-to-run right down to derelict bodies extracted from a field. Geoffrey Claydon was the prime mover in a wise decision, made early on, which ensured that sponsors of any tram coming to Crich had to pay a sum, originally £150, for its depot accommodation, and that once on site, the car would become TMS property. This averted a deluge of 'dead bodies', enabled the TMS to set its own priorities for work and restoration, and avoided the multiplicity of sub-groups and half-finished projects which can still be found today on many railway or bus preservation sites.

Peeling potatoes for use in the members' hut in 1966, left to right, Tim Moore, Martin Miller, Brian King and Jim Jordan.
Mike Crabtree

A proposal by Geoffrey Claydon brought a further step in this direction in May 1963, when a committee was set up to report whether it was practicable or desirable to set an upper limit to the number of cars at the Museum, and what criteria should be applied to determine whether a car should be accepted or retained.

Its report, published on 10 August 1963, drew partly on the experience of its chairman, John Price, as a member of the British Transport Commission's advisory panel on historical relics, and it set out the stages of tramcar development which needed to be portrayed at Crich. In doing so, it made a further significant move towards professional status for this amateur-run museum enterprise. The committee produced a second report in 1978, relating its criteria to the fleet as it then stood, but largely building on the solid work done in 1963.

A third edition was produced in 1988, and this has been taken yet further in a more comprehensive report, placed before the TMS board in 2005. This has been motivated by both past and future considerations. On the one hand, members with first-hand memories of the previous generation of trams were becoming fewer as the years went by, and so it was necessary to write down much background knowledge that previously had been left unrecorded. On the other, a new generation of tramways had emerged in Britain as well as abroad, and the new report needed to prepare for the vintage trams of the future.

A further step towards professional status was taken when the TMS was incorporated as a company limited by guarantee on 17 December 1962. It was also registered as a charity. The company was formed to facilitate the owning of land and to assist limitations of liability. So the unincorporated body established in 1955 was wound up on 30 November 1963 after having transferred all its assets and liabilities to the company. Here again, Geoffrey Claydon played a leading part.

The Museum was now established at Crich. But for the first few years, members still called it "the site". It took some time to adjust to the idea that it was now a museum, open to the public, and not just a construction site. The year 1964 is usually seen as the time when this transition occurred, the year of wonders when electrification took place. But the change really began on 2 June 1963 when Sheffield 15, hauled by a white horse called Bonnie, began a public passenger service over just 200 yards of line. The service continued at weekends for the rest of that season and ran again from April to 28 June 1964.

Fares of 6d (2½p) for adults and 3d (1¼p) for children were charged, traditional-style punch tickets were issued, and an embryo operating department was formed. Crews wore white laboratory coats as uniforms; besides driver and conductor there were usually two assistants to hold the horse's head until the bell was rung for off, and they would then spring back and board the car by the rear platform as it came past. The nearside assistant would learn to avoid banging his head on the oil lamp as he swung aboard; I speak from experience.

Bonnie, who was hired from a neighbouring farmer, Mr Gregory, found Sheffield 15 an easy load. Previously the TMS had for a short time owned its own horse, Felix, who was stabled behind the Cliff Inn, and the first trials with 15 took place as early as 20 October 1962; there had been hopes of running a horse tram service that season. This could have benefited from publicity gained in 1961 when 15 had been borrowed to run on remaining tracks in The Moor, Sheffield, hauled by a horse called Flower. Felix, however, was not happy hauling a tram, had a habit of breaking out of his stable to wander the village at midnight, and eventually found his niche in a Royal Navy shore establishment.

Before the Museum's horse tram service began, visitors were relatively few, and mid-week one could sometimes go for several days without seeing anyone other than members on the site. But the tram service attracted the visitors, and the spare space at Town End began to fill up with their motor cars. Even then, visitors paid no admission charge, and it was to be some years before first a car parking charge and then a combined admission, parking and tram ride charge was made.

Apart from the double track terminal tracks at Town End, which were already in their present form, the single main line was what is now the left-hand, northbound track, filled in with ash up to railhead level as far as a point just north of the old weighbridge house

Johannesburg 60 disguised as Notts & Derby 14 for the Granada Television filming of D H Lawrence's 'Tickets Please' in 1966. The water-based studio paint used was easily washed off afterwards.

Mike Crabtree

(later known as Craft Cottage) to enable the horse to walk on it. Beyond this the track continued with tie bars and sleepers exposed to somewhere near the present Bowes-Lyon Bridge, and two connecting tracks trailed in, one from the stone workshop ('Bacon's curve') and the other from the first tracks of the depot fan. When first laid, much of this main line had been occupied as storage for the trams which kept on arriving, but by early 1963 enough depot space was available to clear the line for running, though several cars were still parked on the southbound track at Town End.

But even while the horse tram service was being organised, preparations for electrification were under way. A quantity of Sheffield poles was acquired and the first was planted on 8 December 1963. Pole erection continued rapidly in the early months of 1964 and immediately transformed the appearance of the site. As one member put it "the place is looking more like an abandoned tramway every week". For as well as the poles, span wires and fittings were erected, using an ex-Grimsby & Immingham rail-mounted tower wagon. Blackpool & Fleetwood 40 had moved under battery power during 1963, and Glasgow works car W21 was set up at the side of the track as a bookshop instead of using the meter house for this purpose.

Memory struggles to recapture the sense of mounting excitement during those early months of 1964. Each week brought new developments; members who had to miss a weekend working there eagerly quizzed those who had the latest news. After four years working in primitive conditions among mud, ballast and mountains of scrap iron, with little apparent progress, all the dreams suddenly seemed to be coming true one after another.

Steam tram engine 'John Bull' with Oporto 9 as trailer prepares to set off up the line on 8 May 1966 on one of its first passenger-carrying journeys at the Museum. Full skirtings enclosing the motion have yet to be fitted

National Tramway Museum / R B Parr

The real transformation of the site took place on Whit Monday, 16 May 1964, when the first trolleywire was erected. A single wire from Town End southbound track, over the crossover and along the northbound track to its limit, it gleamed like a golden filament in the sunlight, a promise of things soon to come. It was energised at low voltage from banks of batteries to allow Blackpool & Fleetwood 2 and generator car 01, the former Sheffield illuminated car 349, to test rail bonds, and at night it carried a.c. current to deter theft.

Meanwhile, the first traction power supply had been set up inside the engine shed at Town End. A motor generator unit, created from two mill motors, took power at 415V a.c. from the village's three-phase supply and gave an output of 160 amps at 406V dc, enough to power one tramcar. Already a diesel generator unit was being installed in 01, using the

Gardner engine from Northern General bus 1105 (GUP105) which was bought for this purpose. But this was not ready in time for the initial electric operation, and so it was the motor generator which first provided traction power at 3 p.m. on 6 June 1964. It placed its heaviest load on the local supply when it was being started up, so this could be done only at off-peak times, when village demands for lighting and cooking were low. At that time the village three-phase supplies were carried on open wires on green-painted tubular steel poles, giving the impression of an abandoned tram route from the Cliff Inn to Crich Common.

London Transport 1 still in the livery of Leeds 301, soon after its arrival from the Museum of British Transport at Clapham.

Mike Crabtree

With careful discipline, one car at a time could be run, and I recall watching the ammeter swing up to 70 amps as Blackpool balcony 40 drew away from Town End, only to fall back as it gathered a modest speed. When public service began on 5 July 1964, it was normally with two cars, loading and starting alternately from each of the two tracks at Town End. Blackpool & Fleetwood 2 was the first in service, and other early performers were 22, Blackpool 40, Fleetwood 40, 45, 49, 59 and 510. Grimsby & Immingham 20 ran in the first season, but not again until it re-emerged as Gateshead 5 in 1966. A ride of about 300 yards was offered.

The first President of the TMS, Chaceley Humpidge, cuts the tape to open the extension to Cabin Crossing on 9 April 1967. With him are Mike Davies and Geoffrey Claydon.

National Tramway Museum / R B Parr

As word spread around of what was happening, the public came, and kept on coming. The electric cars carried 30,687 adults and 15,503 children in 1964, bringing in £1,733 in fares and £8 for private hire. Fares were increased to one shilling adult and 6d children. Services began at noon on Sundays and 2 p.m. on Saturdays, with the season already identified as April to the end of October. Mid-week operation was still something for the future. Because of the short run, conductors were fully occupied collecting fares, so each car carried a three-man crew of driver, conductor and a guard to look after the platform and trolley. The uniform adopted in 1964 was a cream linen jacket, at that time standard summer wear in many offices, with green facings added to the pockets.

Foundations ceremony for the bookshop on 11 September 1966, with Major Charles Walker doing the honours.
National Tramway Museum / R B Parr

It became clear that the single track layout, as well as the power supply, was restricting operation, so during the winter of 1964-65 the main line was doubled to a point short of the present interlaced track. This second, southbound track came into use on 4 April 1965. The single track continued, on the alignment of the present northbound track, to a point a few yards beyond the present bridge, known as Quarry Approach. For a short while cars were fitted with extensions to their destination blinds to display Crich Town End, Quarry Approach or Cliffside, but this practice was soon dropped in favour of destinations from the cars' home towns. Meanwhile the 300 yard Cliffside extension was being built, following the alignment of the former mineral railway towards the quarry, at that time disused and rapidly being overgrown with vegetation. The first car ran on test to Cliffside on 8 March 1965 and passenger service began on 22 May that year.

Opening of the first Extravaganza, with newly-arrived Prague 180 in front of Blackpool 59 carrying the press, a film crew and the band who nearly lost their music!
Mike Crabtree

The intention then was to extend still further into the former quarry, and the track at Cliffside as originally laid curved to the right, pointing in that direction. There was to have been a passing loop shortly beyond this point. However, when modern methods made it economic to reopen the quarry, the new operator, Harry Camm, realised that his proposed stone-crushing plant's location would conflict with the Museum's intended tramway alignment, so his offer was accepted to bulldoze a cutting through the spoilheaps to divert the tramway. The realigned Cliffside terminus came into use on 23 May 1966 and service was extended to Cabin Crossing on 9 April 1967 and to Wakebridge on 25 May 1968.

Steam on all sides at an Extravaganza: The Revd Teddy Boston with his locomotive 'Pixie', the Derby Locomotive Works Society of Model Engineers' miniature railway, and a showman's traction engine with generator in front of its boiler

Ian Yearsley

Although the accent was now firmly on electric operation, 1966 saw the first steam tram operation, using the locomotive John Bull and the Oporto trailer car 9. First steaming of this locomotive had taken place the previous year. Also in 1966 the first full-scale electric traction power supply was commissioned, using a Paxman diesel engine coupled to a Brush generator. This was housed behind the depot buildings, next to what became the workshops. With it was a large bank of ex-trolleybus manoeuvring batteries, providing sufficient power to return the fleet to depot in the event of a power failure. Comment was made at the time that the Paxman engine scarcely changed its note on load, whereas the Gardner 5LW in 01 was often struggling.

Cars of former days on display on the fleamarket site at one of the bank holiday Grand Transport Extravaganza events. This area now forms part of the woodland walk at the Museum

National Tramway Museum

Car parking had to be rearranged at this time. Land with space for 200 cars had been purchased in 1964 for £3,000, alongside the main Museum site and providing a new entrance from the highway to the east of the existing one. With the reopening of the quarry, the car park had to be redesigned and a perimeter road created for the quarry traffic. Visitors at this time could come in direct from the main road, as the entrance had no gates, but from the car park they came down steps near the bookshop and the present staff entrance, until 1967 when a sloping path was constructed leading down behind the oil store (the former weighbridge house) alongside the track towards what is now Stephenson Place near the bookshop. This path was fenced, for the double track of the main line was then ballasted to railhead and crossing was allowed only at Stephenson Place where the ash surface used by the horse cars had been retained and extended. For some years there was even a fence between up and down lines here, to prevent passengers crossing into the path of moving cars.

The path was the first of the recommendations to be carried out of the Tramways Sub-Committee's report, issued in April 1967. This examined visitor circulation and the scene within which the trams were presented and operated. Up to then we had produced a tramway infrastructure and got trams moving on it, but there operated against a background of uneven ground, parked trams, sheds and vegetation. It was not evident to many visitors that trams originally ran along urban streets. The Sub-Committee's terms of reference were to consider how to create an authentic British tramway atmosphere. It recommended that the area around the double track be built up as an urban street scene, and specific proposals included a stone bridge at the north end, a depot boundary wall, park railings, pavements, facades to the depots, the surfacing of the depot yard and floors, and a variety of shops and public buildings on the street and facing the 'market place' created at Town End. Most of its recommendations, one way or another, have been carried out, though the parade of shops along the street and the monument suggested for Town End have not yet taken shape. Nevertheless, the Assembly Rooms, the Red Lion, The Burnley Tramways Offices, the Yorkshire Penny Bank and many items of street furniture were acquired in fulfilment of this concept.

'Extravaganza' back-drop of fairground rides as Sheffield 189 heads north and crowds fill the Fleamarket area.
Ian Yearsley

One important principle it laid down was that buildings should be no later than Edwardian in character, so that any period from 1901 onwards could be depicted. It also suggested that the original Guildcrete structure Depot A should be re-sited to serve an upper level line, possibly horse-operated, in the car park area. A further proposal was for a mixed gauge line of Irish 5ft. 3in. and Continental metre gauge with its own depot at Derwent View, the far end of the present traverser pit.

Setting the scene

The Tramways Sub-Committee of the TMS, in its report of April 1967, put forward various ideas for creating an Edwardian street scene around the tramway at Crich. At that time the Society had only just begun to collect the facades of original buildings, several of which today flank the street, though the original stone buildings were in place. The scenes as imagined then, however, bear a remarkable resemblance to what exists today. Drawings by the author are reproduced from the 1999 Annual Report and from 'Ten Years at Crich'.

The bridge, the footpath with park railings, and the depot yard wall were all envisaged in 1967, though the timekeeper's hut never came to be.

Not quite the Red Lion, but at this stage a pub was envisaged on the other side of the road, while a chapel would lead into a row of arcaded shops.

The track layout was not quite like this at Town End, but the Birmingham shelter is recognisable. One feature which has never come to fruition is the monument, rather like a war memorial, on which could be inscribed the names of tramway pioneers. And the building lightly sketched in on the left; was this a hint of the Derby Assembly Rooms facade to come?

The years 1967 to 1971 brought significant developments at the Museum. Some of them demonstrated what could be done by volunteer labour, others showed the need for full-time staff. All of them enhanced the professionalism of the Museum and its organisation, and so brought credit to the TMS and its members.

The Revd. Teddy Boston, from Cadeby, and the Revd. Gordon Bathie, vicar of Crich, lead the Crich parish choir to the bandstand for an Extravaganza Sunday service. Glasgow 22 has been inserted into the service to bring them; its crew have already turned the pole for it to return

Ian Yearsley

During 1967 an idea was developed by Winstan Bond to recreate an old-time bank holiday scene, complete with a steam fairground, old vehicles and a flea market, to be built around the tramway for the 1968 August Bank Holiday weekend. The proprietor of Old Motor magazine, Prince Marshall, was brought in with a team of his colleagues to organise the fair and vintage vehicles. Prince himself was no stranger to Crich, for earlier on he had proposed that the Historic Commercial Vehicle Club (HCVC) should establish a bus museum alongside. This would have included trolleybuses powered from the tramway supply but run by the HCVC; but the opportunity was not taken up.

At that time shows on this scale were still rare, and the Bank Holiday event planned for the Museum had so many facets that the title chosen, 'Grand Transport Extravaganza', did not seem out of place. Already it seemed set to be the biggest thing that had happened at Crich, but events elsewhere thrust it on to the international stage.

A busy scene at Town End on 27 May 1966. Sheffield 330 prepares to water the track, with Southampton 45 well-loaded with passengers behind. Generator car 01 stands on the west track feeding power to the overhead line.

National Tramway Museum / R B Parr

A year before this, some engineers from CKD, the Czechoslovak tramcar builder, had visited the Museum and were so impressed by it that they persuaded their company to restore a Prague tramcar of 1905 and present it to the TMS. Its journey was so timed that it could be formally handed over at the opening of the Extravaganza on 1 September 1968; it left Prague on a CKD tramcar delivery lorry on 19 August, and by the following day it had reached Germany. During the next night, Soviet troops invaded Czechoslovakia, and immediately the historic tramcar became a national symbol. It arrived at Crich on 30 August and the five CKD engineers winched it down the ramp from their lorry, raised the trolleypole, and immediately set off up the line, leaving a crowd of surprised members at Town End. These engineers did not know at that time whether they would be able to return to their own country, let alone what they would find on their tram ride up the quarry.

But they were all there, in sober suits, when Dr Frantisek Horak, Commercial Attache at the Czechoslovak Embassy, stood alongside George Brown, the local Member of Parliament, as he declared the Extravaganza open. There was nearly a hitch at this point, for the local colliery band on the top deck of Blackpool 59 had lost their music for the Czechoslovak national anthem, but it was found with minutes to spare and the anthems of the United Kingdom and Czechoslovakia rang out. The Revd. Teddy Boston from Cadeby and the Revd. Gordon Bathie, vicar of Crich, conducted a short church service from the front platform of Sheffield 15. Then, with the band playing 'Congratulations', and photographers and a film crew perched on the rear stairs, 59 moved off, followed by Prague 180 driven by George Brown, and so set in motion not only the 1968 Extravaganza, but a whole series of Extravaganzas that continued until the end of the 1980s and even after that on a reduced scale as the Crich Transport Gathering. A film entitled 'Extravaganza' commemorates the 1968 event and the arrival of Prague 180, with Janacek's 'Symphonietta' as theme music and George Brown's speech as commentary.

And what a show it was in 1968: the steam fair occupied the car park, flea market stalls and old vehicles covered the hills on the western side of the tracks behind the present bandstand area, and fields round about were hired for car parking. For this first year, police set up a one-way traffic system round Crich village. Everywhere was music, colour, lights, smells of steam, hot oil and roast chestnuts. The people came in their thousands. And then the heavens opened; a torrential downpour brought the fairground to a standstill and visitors scurrying for shelter. But the trams kept on running, and conductors kept on collecting fares. The team of 150 members who staffed the show for the TMS showed the fairground professionals that this could be done, even by volunteers, and a new respect developed.

Open trackwork in the early 1960s. Glasgow 1282, Sheffield 510, Blackpool 49 and 167, and Glasgow 22 before erection of overhead on the main line.
Mike Crabtree

Extravaganzas over the years included many attractions: balloon ascents, fly-pasts of historic and aerobatic aircraft, a narrow gauge railway, rides on open-platform Paris buses, a narrow-gauge horse tramway on the fleamarket site. The 20,000 visitors of 1968 rose to 33,000 by the 1973 Extravaganza of whom 20,080 rode on the trams, but numbers then declined gradually as attractions elsewhere developed, though the weekend remained a huge social event for members. It is safe to say that no one who has ever driven, conducted or acted as marshal in the Extravaganza crowds will forget the experience, the queues for tram rides extending from Town End into Stephenson Place and beyond, or the sheer carnival atmosphere of the event.

Somewhat overshadowed by all these events, a new permanent bookshop opened, replacing the sales outlet in Glasgow works car W21. This building also included gents and ladies toilets, though these had to be supplemented at busy times by temporary facilities, hired-in. One Extravaganza story is of an inspector at Town End who took pity on a long queue of ladies waiting to use the toilet behind the bookshop. He commandeered Sheffield 189, loaded the ladies into it, and sent it up the line to where temporary toilets were provided. Some confusion with the single line staffs caused the car to be delayed, and afterwards the crew, ashen-faced, described the growing wrath of their trapped and anxious passengers as the moments ticked by.

Operating the tramway

Right from the start, it was always the plan that some of the trams in the collection should be operated for the benefit and enjoyment of visitors. Initial ideas indicated that a couple of trams running a few trips on a summer Sunday afternoon would suffice. A Traffic Department was set up, and operating methods and practices developed following traditional tramway practice as far as possible. Tickets of traditional tramway type are used, with 'Bell Punches' but other ticket equipment (Ultimate and TIM) can be used on the (historically) appropriate trams. All platform staff and inspectors wear tramway period uniforms. Fares are collected by roving conductors on the tram and passengers are expected to board and alight at the proper stopping places using the correct end of the tram. Discipline is also traditional, and woe betide the conductor whose waybill doesn't balance or the driver with destination screens, platform chains, lights or saloon seats incorrectly set, or trolley not turned.

The original 'summer Sunday' operating concept has now grown far beyond expectations into running a tramway for 250 days every year with upwards of three trams each day, with all the attendant maintenance and infrastructure demands. The busiest weekend ever, the August 1978 Extravaganza, the first Bank Holiday after the Glory Mine extension opened, required a 14-tram service which, at the peak, resulted in 56 movements an hour through Wakebridge loop for over three hours in the afternoon, with 1,750 passengers an hour each way, to dissolve the queues at all the stops. The tram service operated from 7.15 a.m. to 11.54 p.m. throughout this Bank Holiday period, such was the demand. The Museum's maximum year for visitors was 1978, although Extravaganza attendances had already reached their peak. The queue for tram rides in that year stretched from Town End terminus to a point beyond the present engineering gallery. As recorded elsewhere, volunteer input by TMS members remains crucial to the success of the Museum.

An equally complex piece of tramway operating, though without such passenger demands, occurs each year in the 'Tramathon' on the day following the Annual General Meeting and President's Evening of the Society. This can trace its origins to a Members' Day parade on 8 May 1966, when despite the limitations of the Gardner-bus-engined power supply from car 01, a procession of nine cars was run. Cars were driven up to Cliffside one by one, and then coasted down at regular intervals, thus providing, as the TMS Journal put it, "a tram spectacular on limited means". The choreography of these events on its own is a major task.

Information supplied by **Malcolm Wright.**

Also at this time the opening sequence of Ken Russell's award-winning production of D H Lawrence's 'Women in Love' was filmed at the Museum. Over the years the Museum has been used as the setting for a number of feature films and television productions, with Stephenson Place transformed variously into a market place with stalls and a shopping street in Manchester, and cars disguised with studio paint.

Above: The facade of the Derby Assembly Rooms just before it was dismantled for re-erection at the Museum.
Jonathan Johansson Collection

Right: Derby Assembly Rooms, again at the Museum; by 1975 the lavatories were in use but not until 1982 could the upper floors be used to house the library.
Jonathan Johansson Collection

Manchester 765 operated at the Museum in 1977-78; here it prepares to depart from Town End for Wakebridge.
Mike Crabtree

The years from 1968 to 1971 were a time of spectacular growth for the Museum. Gross income jumped from £6,000 to £21,000, then to £27,000 and £32,000. Writing in the Journal in 1972, Winstan Bond attributed this to the new bookshop, the Extravaganza, the doubling of tram fares on Sundays to 2s (10p) adults and 1s (5p) child, and the 1s charge at the car park. Admission charges were introduced in 1973.

Gleaming ballast on the main line with Gateshead 5, Manchester 765 and Vienna 4225, later restored as New York Third Avenue 674.

Ian Yearsley

The 1968 Annual Report was the first to appear in the booklet format which has continued, much improved, to the present day. It showed a turnover of £21,235, more than three times the previous year. Illustrations included the first set of depot doors, wooden with windows at the top, but Merlyn Bacon, by then chief tramways engineer, warned that the fleet was deteriorating because of insufficient maintenance, unskilled work and unsatisfactory working conditions.

The committee had become the Board of Management in April 1966, and its members that year were Chaceley Humpidge (president), Geoff Hyde (chairman), Geoffrey Claydon (vice-chairman and secretary), Merlyn Bacon, Winstan Bond, Vic Chatburn, Michael Davis, John Edgar, George Hearse, Jim Jordan, John Markham, John Marsh, Maurice O'Connor, David Senior, Charles Walker and Michael Ward. Basil Miller had been chairman until the previous year and Martin S Miller was minutes secretary. Ian Musgrove had been appointed editor to recommence publication of the Journal following a brief experiment with 'Tramway Topics'. He was succeeded by Steve Palmer.

Treasure to be sorted at the back of a roller-towel laundry in Catford, London, where British Electric Traction Company archives were stored. TMS members and Museum staff carry out many off-site tasks such as this.

Ian Yearsley

Up to the mid-1960s, members seeking economically-priced accommodation on-site often slept in the cars, but with numbers increasing both of members and visitors, this was becoming impractical. So an initiative led by Winstan Bond in 1965 resulted in a 'Members' Hut' being built. This was promptly christened 'The Crich Hilton' and it could and often did provide sleeping bag space for up to 20 members on the floor. Cooking, washing and even slide-shows were possible. Memories such as those of balancing a mug of hot water on 812's controller while shaving using the driver's mirror began to fade. This hut lasted for nearly 30 years and its many facets were celebrated eloquently in a letter by Jim Jordan in the April 1992 TMS Journal.

The Crich village bus: My Lady Coaches of Crich Common operated two Bedford OBs in brown livery on a Saturday-only service to Ripley, filling-in between the Trent departures, in the early 1960s

Mike Crabtree

Volunteers at the 1969 Extravaganza were the first to use another hut, the 'tea hut', now the tea rooms, which replaced the tea caravan previously located near Town End. I was one of a team which served 50 cooked breakfasts a day in this building, newly-erected and still not fitted-out, apart from kitchen equipment. A feature of its first furniture was seats from Metro-Cammell railway coaches intended for Rhodesia but prevented by sanctions then in force from being exported. But it was not until 1976 that the Society assumed responsibility for the Museum refreshment services.

This request stop, rarely used, was provided to give the tramway fiscal status of a transport provider. Sheffield 264 passes, southbound.

Ian Yearsley

1969 also saw the start of mid-week operation, on Tuesdays, Wednesdays and Thursdays and at first only "by prior arrangement for parties"; by 1970 this had become a regular feature. The practice of volunteers bunking down in tramcars had already ceased, though workers at the Extravaganza and some other busy times still camped out on the site. But in 1970 two houses were bought and combined to form Field House, and in 1973 Field Cottage was acquired. In future these properties were to provide accommodation for members. Conditions were becoming more civilised, and a wash at the end of a day's work no longer meant heating a kettle on a camping stove.

The long tradition of illuminated trams to celebrate times of rejoicing has been revived many times at the Museum, and here members bask in the glow of lights on Blackpool works car 2 on an Extravaganza evening

Ian Yearsley

Away from the Museum, a lease was taken on a railway building at Clay Cross, previously used as a store for surplus and unrestored vehicles by the BTC. Over the years since then it has provided the same service to the TMS, as well as giving space at one time to some preserved buses. The freehold of this building has now been acquired.

By this time the need for better maintenance, signalled in the 1966 report, was becoming urgent. Until 1969, the only inspection pit for routine maintenance was formed from the foundations of the former powder magazine in the approach tracks to Depot IV, roads 10, 11 and 12. It was so small that only one bogie at a time could be dealt with, and cars would have to be shunted. And it was open to wind and rain.

New folding doors reveal London Transport 1 and Leicester 76; tracks 12, 13 and 14 still have the old sliding doors.

Ian Yearsley

A new bay of Atcost construction, completed in 1963-66 on the east side of the main depot complex and intended originally for storage tracks, was earmarked instead as a workshop, with two tracks instead of three. The first section of pit was completed in 1968 and early in 1971 the original Depot A was dismantled to allow the workshop to be extended forward to its full length. Unlike most preserved railways, we did not inherit any workshop facilities but had to build our own, and it was the largest civil engineering task we had carried out as volunteers. Not only did parts of the two pits have to be drilled or blasted out of solid rock, but since the crane could not be used (there was no track to run it on) the long lengths of RSJs which serve as the base for the running rails flanking the pits had to be manually installed. Up to forty persons per RSJ were needed to lift them into place. The floors had to be capable of taking the weight of trams when lifted on jacks, and the work also consumed the largest quantities of ready-mixed concrete ever used on site, and it had to be cast both on the horizontal and (for the pit sides) vertical planes. But at last maintenance work could go on under cover, with heating in winter, and the way was opened for a new approach to restoration as well. On the main depots themselves, folding doors replaced the wooden sliding doors in 1974 and the floors were fully concreted. But it was not until 1976 that overhead wires were erected inside the depots, ending the tricky process of shunting cars in and out with pairs of bamboo poles linked by jumper cables.

Less obviously to the visitor, another major change was taking place, for in 1971 the first full-time employee was engaged. Full-time staff remained few in number until 1976 when the first job-creation scheme brought a team of craftsmen, government-funded but requiring TMS staff to supervise. This made restoration possible on a seven-days-a-week basis, with volunteers at weekends and employees on weekdays sharing the same facilities.

Before the bridge was built, the staff post was here. Leeds 180 heads south followed by Glasgow 1100, while Glasgow 812 and Blackpool 49, then in red livery, wait their turn.

Ian Yearsley

More apparent to the visitor was the construction of the Assembly Rooms' facade, transferred from Derby Market Place, with foundations laid at the Museum in 1972. Part of it was used for an exhibition in 1974, lavatories were built in it in 1975, and by 1982 it became possible to develop the upper floors as a library, film archive and photographic department. June 1972 also saw the erection of the Birmingham shelter at Town End, though the area round it was at that time still paved with packed earth. In the same month, the first stage of the Peak District Mines Historical Society's replica lead mine was completed at Wakebridge. Already the Museum was taking on much of the aspect we know today.

Richard Fairburn keeps an eye on the service operations at Town End while passengers queue for tramcars.
Ian Yearsley

Mission Statement

The mission of the National Tramway Museum is:

- To maintain and develop an operating tramway museum for the benefit of the nation.

- To create an attractive and historically appropriate environment around the tramway.

- To exhibit to the public as many representative aspects of tramway heritage as is practically and historically appropriate.

- To create and develop an archive and library of national importance.

- To be an internationally recognised centre of excellence in all fields of tramway heritage.

In 1975 the Duke of Gloucester became Patron of the Society following interest shown by his late brother, Prince William, and the Duke paid his first visit on 5 June 1976. This was to be the first of several visits, formal and informal, and he continues to take a close interest in the way the Museum develops.
David Frodsham

In 1978, thanks to another job creation scheme, the tramway was extended to a new terminus at Glory Mine, giving a total run of one mile and opening up dramatic views of the Derwent Valley. This extension on leased land was opened on 7 July 1978 by the Rt.. Hon. Albert Booth MP, Secretary of State for Employment, and on the same day the new Wakebridge substation and viewing gallery were brought into use. From then on the main traction power supply was through an ex-Walsall 250 kW silicon rectifier at Wakebridge, backed up when necessary by the Paxman diesel generator behind the workshop and a rotary converter unit which came from the London Brick Company.

The Museum was also making use of new technology; information was made available in 1978 on the Prestel service to television viewers, and a free service was offered to other museums. It was then hard to imagine that by 1997 images from the photographic collection would be available on the World Wide Web.

An animated scene with Leicester 76 in service as Blackpool 40 in green livery heads north past the partly-completed Assembly Rooms facade.
Mike Crabtree

The following year, 1979, saw the former quarry foreman's house converted to provide proper administrative accommodation with a full-time secretary and bookkeeper and even a photocopier. Upstairs, one room was used as the traffic office, where drivers and conductors signed on and off duty. Named 'Poplar House', it now commemorates Gladys Poplar who occupied it during the developing years of the Museum.

Glasgow 1297 operating with a trolley pole, at Anchorsholme in, July 1985.
Mike Crabtree

Following completion of the library building in 1982, a full-time librarian and a photographic archivist were appointed in 1983. And so workshops, library, staff, expertise, growing confidence and financial stability paved the way for a series of ventures which in the next two decades took trams from Crich to operate on tracks elsewhere. The 1985 centenary celebrations of Blackpool Tramways resulted in eight cars being loaned, including the steam tram engine; meanwhile two Blackpool cars came to the Museum for the season to help with traffic and to make space in their own depot for the visiting cars.

The Garden Festival at Glasgow in 1988 was an even greater effort, for this involved advice on setting up a tramway, training staff to run it, and supplying trams. Contracts were drawn up, and cars 22, 68 and 1297 went from the Museum, along with an open boat car from Blackpool and Edinburgh 35 from Lothian Regional Transport. The tramway ran for 152 days and carried 1.56 million passengers including the Prince and Princess of Wales, the Duke of Edinburgh, the Prime Minister and Denis Thatcher.

Consultancy was provided and trams loaned to the Gateshead Garden Festival in 1990, and the intention was to send Gateshead 5, Newcastle 102 and Sunderland 100 as cars of local interest, but problems with 5 led to 167 taking its place. Replacement cars could be required at short notice under these contracts, which were made for commercial reasons through a separate company, TMS Enterprises Ltd..

Site workers consult as the bandstand from Longford Park, Stretford, takes shape.
Ian Yearsley

One of the briefest operations ever by a car from the Museum was by horse car 15 in its native city in 1995 as part of the celebrations for the completion of the Sheffield Supertram network. Not only was it exhibited at Kelham Island Industrial Museum from July to November, but on 17 October it was brought out to perform one trip in the city centre. A slightly longer visit in 1998 was by Blackpool & Fleetwood 2 and Blackpool 167 to their home town for the Fleetwood centenary on 12 July.

All these events have generated funds and enthusiasm for cars to be restored, most notably in the case of Metropolitan 331, which ran for a short time in Sunderland colours until British Steel sponsored it in an all-over blue livery for the Gateshead event.

Towering above all these achievements was a project, launched in 1986, to create an exhibition hall, facing depots V and VI of the existing depot complex with access by a traverser. This hall was designed to give more space both for viewing tramcars and to avoid damage to paintwork by prams, rucksacks and umbrellas of visitors squeezing past them. Externally it was to look like a traditional tram depot, but internally it was arranged to replicate one of the great tramway exhibitions of the early twentieth century, with components as well as cars displayed on manufacturers' stands.

Support for The TMS and its Museum

The Tramway Museum Society has worked with a number of partners to carry out its aims. Several organisations dedicated to tramcar restoration work closely with the TMS to fund work in the NTM workshops and elsewhere.

The Tramcar Sponsorship Organisation, dating from 1961, has raised funds for the acquisition, transport and restoration of trams at the NTM. Cars 2, 7, 74, 167 and the Brill snowbroom have all received funding from the TSO, which also paid the purchase and transport costs of 273 whose restoration was funded by the Heritage Lottery Fund.

London County Council Tramways Trust for many years had its own workshop at Bonwell Street, London, where restoration work on 102 and 1622 was carried out before completion at NTM. It bought Lisbon bogies for London United Tramways 159, now in the workshops at NTM for its LCCT-funded restoration.

Scottish Tramways and Transport Society has supported various projects and worked with Merseyside Transport Preservation Society to fund the restoration of Liverpool 869. The Fylde Tramway Society and the Leeds Transport Historical Society have also supported restoration projects.

Grants became a significant item in the Tramway Museum Society accounts from 1992 onwards, with the Heritage Lottery Fund playing a major part from 1998. East Midlands Museum Service, the Museums, Libraries and Archives Council (including Prism grants in 1995 and 2003), the Carnegie UK Trust, Resource, DEFRA/Countryside Agency, the Transport History Research Trust, Amber Valley Borough Council and the Department for Education and Skills have all made important contributions.

These have been variously for building projects, tramcar restoration, information technology, conservation, education, and publicity. In earlier years the government Job Creation schemes provided valuable personnel, and several were also provided by Swedish job creation schemes. All of them involved considerable administrative input by TMS members.

Bequests have been on a generous scale in the past decade especially.

Blackpool 40, still in green livery, loads at Town End while Glasgow 22's crew take their lunch break The shelter has yet to come.

Ian Yearsley

Even more distinctive was the method of financing this major project. In part it was supported by the Tramcar Sponsorship Organisation, but a major part of the more than £200,000 was raised through development debentures from members, employees and their families. Subscribers could choose between 0%, 5% and 10% fixed rate interest, and the debentures were repayable over the period 1992 to 2006, so that today only a small number are outstanding. As the original prospectus pointed out, borrowing

Gateshead 5 reverses at Wakebridge with the Glory Mine extension under construction ahead.
Ian Yearsley

commercially would have exposed the Museum to risks and high interest charges.

At that time of high inflation ordinary investors could get 14% interest on a long term loan outside, and even the 10% fixed rate interest involved some sacrifice for members who subscribed, though as inflation and interest rates fell the debentures became an excellent investment.

As well as the main exhibition hall, there was an annex, originally intended to house a power station display but latterly used to great effect as a children's area. Provision of wet-weather space for visitors was an important feature of the plan, and the hall added 16,500 sq.ft. of covered space to the 18,000 sq. ft. of the depots. It also reduced fire risk, by being a separate building. Work began on the exhibition hall in 1987 and it was formally inaugurated by Sir Neil Cossons, director of the Science Museum, in 1991. One incidental use of the building was for holding social events such as the annual president's evening which eventually replaced the more formal annual dinner held in a hotel in Matlock or Derby.

Glasgow 22 in the depot at the Glasgow Garden Festival in 1988. Behind it is Glasgow 1297 and alongside is a 'boat' car from Blackpool. Tram track was laid for the duration of the Festival.
Mike Crabtree

By any standard, the Society's achievements at the Museum are impressive. They include the opening of the Bowes-Lyon bridge by the Minister of State for Transport in 1988; registered status as a national museum in 1990 (the title National Tramway Museum had been adopted at the end of 1980); freeholds of the line to Wakebridge acquired in 1982 and to Glory Mine in 1996, the same year that the four millionth visitor arrived and the project to digitise the photographic collection began. 1993 brought 68 people to the Museum for the second symposium of the Roads and Road Transport History Association and in November 1997, in an even more bold venture, the Society co-operated with the University of York's Institute of Railway Studies in organising a 'Suburbanising the Masses' conference at the National Railway Museum, York, which brought together historians of transport and town planning from several countries. The same year brought Designation status, a mark of excellence among museums which helps greatly when applying for grants. Two years later, the Museum contributed to the IRS distance learning project on the history of urban transport. The TMS has also taken the lead in the educational exercise 'Learning on the Move', jointly with the National Railway Museum, the National Motor Museum, the National Waterways Museum and London's Transport Museum. Historical knowledge of TMS members also played a part in the British Film Institute and University of Sheffield project during 2003-2005 to restore Edwardian era films in the Mitchell & Kenyon collection.

Rooftop view at Wakebridge as Liverpool 869 and Glasgow 1282 wait to pass Leeds 180

Ian Yearsley

Inauguration of the Access Tram, Berlin 3006, on 26 April 1997, to provide facilities for the disabled, was another milestone, and its success has led to purchase of another suitable tramcar for conversion with a wheelchair lift, Halle 902, a double-ended version of the widely-used CKD design.

This takes us into the present decade, from the mid-1990s to the year 2005 when the TMS celebrates its 50-year jubilee. On the one hand this has been a period clouded by various worries about visitor numbers, taxation and finance, resulting even in some measures of retrenchment. On the other hand it has been a period of growth, with important new buildings, developments and tramcar restorations.

Throughout the 1970s, visitor numbers were routinely about 150,000. This steadily declined until in 2000 visitors were at their lowest number since 1967, at around 75,000. As the 2003 annual report put it: "The reason is well documented - intense competition for the leisure pound in the form of Sunday shopping, designer outlets and more attractions." There seemed a gloomy inevitability about this, but then the trend was reversed, with visitor numbers rising by 25% in 2001 and continuing to rise, albeit less spectacularly, through 2002 into 2003 when there were 105,000 visitors. This represented an overall 40% rise on the 2000 figures. However, 2004's figures were down on 2003 and at the time of writing, May 2005, visitors were down by 10% on 2004.

Staying independent

This heading comes from a special issue of the TMS newsletter 'Contact' issued in August 1986 to explain to members and staff the consequences of a long period with visitors below the 100,000 a year level. Winstan Bond, the treasurer, said that the break-even point in finances was a result of three factors: the number of visitors, the income from the visitors, and the total expenses. A graph begun in 1974 showed the healthy distance which the break-even point maintained beneath the visitor numbers until 1986 when they came together. Instead of having money for capital expenditure at the Museum, were this to continue there would not even be enough to pay the running costs.

Visitor numbers continued to decline into the 1990s, although money spent per visitor at the Museum increased. But the re-branding exercise arrested the trend, and for a while visitors started to increase again towards the 115,000 regarded as a comfortable break-even level.

Meanwhile, in 1996, the government unexpectedly imposed Value Added Tax (VAT) on tram rides. To counter this, Gift Aid on admissions was actively promoted by the Inland Revenue and adopted by the Museum; this covered most of the increase in the cost base. A whole programme of special events, from 'Thomas the Tank Engine' days to World War 2 weekends has enhanced revenue as well as raising the profile of the Society and its Museum.

Another time-consuming but often rewarding task has been to make submissions for awards by grant-making bodies. Sometimes much time and effort is expended only to find that the rules have changed and the process has to be started all over again. Nevertheless the Society has gained very significant financial support for its projects through these efforts and one of the most heartening developments is that at least one major grant-making body will now give value to voluntary hours of labour as matching funds in assessing grants.

The task of the Board and its Treasurer in piloting a way through these obstacles is not an easy one. But the Society has been fortunate over the years in finding people with ability and professional knowledge to serve on its Board and the various committees. Less glamorous than the tasks immediately linked with the trams and their physical infrastructure, their work nevertheless not only enables the trams to keep running, but ensures that the Museum is not dependent on bank loans to see it through each winter season.

Based on material drawn from 'Contact' August 1986 and TMS Annual Reports 1999, 2001 and 2003.

Liverpool 869 and Glasgow 1282 both display L plates as they offer the ultimate tram driving experience. A careful watch is kept as the car moves on to the crossover

Ian Yearsley

One factor in the visitor increase of 2001, sadly, was that the countryside's misfortune, the foot and mouth epidemic, aided the Museum in early months of the year when so many competing attractions were forced to close down or to welcome only those visitors prepared to wade through trays of disinfectant. But the Board had already adopted a self-help policy which resulted in a series of new events to attract visitors, followed by a 're-branding' of the Museum as the Crich Tramway Village and a series of television advertisements. It worked, and it gives pointers for future efforts.

A rise in visitor numbers to at least 115,000 is needed to ensure long-term financial viability, but the experience of 2001 has shown that moves towards this are possible, and unlike some other museums and preserved lines the Society is not dependent on bank loans to see it through the winter months. Our continued viability is possible only because the Museum is attractive to visitors, many of whom are looking for a family day out rather than specifically to look at trams. All this requires personnel: by the summer of 2003 the number of full time staff had risen to 24, supplemented by about another 24 part time seasonal staff. Volunteer input by Society members remains crucial to the success of the Museum, however, and the recorded input from the 230 or so active volunteer members in 2004 was estimated to be the equivalent of no fewer than 32 employees. As well as activities at Crich, there are 17 area organisers concerned with events and activities in their own areas; two of these areas are outside Britain. And certainly being a member of the TMS will assure a welcome at museum and heritage tramways right across the world, from Ferrymead in New Zealand to the Open Air Museum in Arnhem, Netherlands.

The appearance of the Museum's Edwardian street scene was transformed by several new buildings from the late 1990s onwards. Work began in 2001 on a workshop extension with viewing gallery enabling the public for the first time to see the work of restoration and maintenance in progress which opened in 2002. It occupied the site of the former car wash bay, concealed behind an advertisement hoarding. Across the street, the Red Lion pub from Stoke on Trent had slowly been taking shape throughout the 1990s, much of it by volunteer labour and fully funded by the Museum; in March 2002 it opened, giving new vistas on the street and providing a venue for many social occasions. Its traditional bar downstairs, recently extended, is matched by the high quality of restaurant facilities upstairs; thanks to a ramp constructed from the tearooms, both floors at the Red Lion are fully accessible. It looks across the street to the Forge Bookshop, with a range of stock for visitors and enthusiasts alike.

Workshops procedures are explained in the course of a conductor training day. Cars visible are Blackpool 40 and Liverpool 869

Isabelle O'Brien

Preparing for a cavalcade: Edinburgh 35 will follow Paisley 68, LCC 106, Newcastle 102 and Southampton 45, showing the great difference in height between the four open top cars
Ian Yearsley

Work started in 2002 on the Library extension, incorporating facades of the Burnley Tramways Office and the Yorkshire Penny Bank from Nelson, Lancashire. This was completed in 2003 and inaugurated on 14 April by the Duke of Gloucester. The greatly-extended library has been named to commemorate John Price, who over the years contributed largely to the historical study of tramways. Besides providing much-needed library, archive and reading room space, it includes meeting rooms and offices, and early in 2005 the Museum's headquarters offices moved from Poplar House to the Burnley Tramways Office. Meanwhile a woodland walk and sculpture trail which had been created parallel with the tramway as far as Wakebridge was opened; for many people this provided an attraction as fascinating as the trams themselves.

Restored as a static exhibit in the Exhibition Hall, Derby 1 is here having lettering completed on its lower deck. It now forms pride of place on the Brush display stand in the Tramways Exhibition
Ian Yearsley

Tramcar restorations went ahead too. Sheffield 74 emerged in 1995, London 1622 in 1996, Chesterfield 7 in 1997 and Oporto 273 in 2000. This year Leeds 345 is nearing completion and London United 159 has arrived as the next restoration candidate in the Workshop. It is possible now for a visitor to find four trams running, none of which he would have been able to see ten years ago, among buildings which did not exist then. In addition, work has continued to carry out routine though sometimes quite extensive overhauls and to maintain cars in service. This needs to be set against criticisms that there are cars which have not turned a wheel in service for many years. Consistently, sometimes against great odds, the Workshops has provided an average of 17 cars each year for service for the past 30 years. The great majority of the fleet have run at some time or another; to maintain the whole fleet in running order at all times would require workshops and staff three times the size of the present establishment. There is however a problem with depot space and from time to time various cars have to be transferred to store and more will probably have to follow if and when further cars arrive.

The TMS today is the proprietor of an enterprise with a turnover of £1.8 million. In man-hours, work by volunteers still exceeds that of full-time staff and a great deal of work is done off-site as well as at the Museum. But the members' subscriptions and donations

The TMS badge, SHMD 62

Very early on in the history of the Tramway Museum Society, its publicity officer, Dennis Gill, commissioned a drawing from one of his former Mather and Platt colleagues, Harry Butterworth, of Stalybridge, Hyde, Mossley and Dukinfield Joint Board car 62. Harry Butterworth was an artist who among other things designed tea-towels, and he worked from photographs supplied to him. Dennis chose this car as being a typical car which might have been a candidate for preservation had it still existed; he deliberately avoided choosing any car which was or might form part of the TMS fleet. This car, with its surrounding garter, was then adopted as the TMS badge.

So what was the history of this car? Following a prototype, no 24, built in 1921, cars 61 and 62 were built at the SHMD's Park Road works, Stalybridge, in 1924, replacing two of the cars taken over in 1921 from the Oldham, Ashton and Hyde company. Two more similar cars, Nos. 63 and 64, followed a year later. All were built as low-height cars to enable them to work to Stockport and Edgeley, which they did regularly from 1925, although they also had Manchester-style stencil indicators to enable them to work on the joint Hyde-Manchester service, no 19, in which SHMD cars had shared from 1923 onwards.

These SHMD cars had been designed throughout as low-height vehicles and they did not have the squat appearance of Stockport low-height cars on the same route which had been created by adding low-height top covers to existing standard-height lower decks. During the second world war the four

cars 61-64, with Nos. 18 and 42, worked from the remaining SHMD depot at Lewis Street, Hyde until the end of the Joint Board's tramway operation in 1945. Known locally as 'green linnets' because of their dark green and white livery, these cars ended their days being converted into holiday homes at Godley, near Hyde. Part of the dash of no 18, showing the dark green livery, white lining out and gold numerals, is exhibited at the Heaton Park tramway in Manchester.

Information on the car's history is taken from the book SHMD Joint Board, by WGS Hyde and E Ogden, Stockport Corporation Tramways by Maurice Marshall, and from the author's own recollections of seeing the cars in service before 1945 and at Godley in 1948.

item in the accounts, which formed 100% of income in the 1950s, now forms less than 8%, despite the fact that membership has grown from 65 to more than 2,500. Much of the income now comes from operating the Museum, including catering and retail sales, as well as grants. Understandably, members from time to time feel that the enterprise they have created is now out of their control, and this has found expressions in protests at the annual general meeting. But step by step, incorporation, charity status, and all the commitments to excellence which have culminated in Designation status, have alongside their benefits brought demands which require the Museum to be run to professional standards. All this is in addition to the ever-increasing safety standards imposed by legislation and by codes of practice drawn up by the Health & Safety Executive.

The Roads and Road Transport History Association held its first symposium at the Museum in 1993; 68 delegates stand in front of Sheffield 510 and Trent's preserved bus. On the right, the Red Lion begins to take shape.
National Tramway Museum/Glynn Wilton

Failed in traffic: the Blackpool locomotive shunts Southampton 45 into the workshops for attention after the crew report a problem with the car in service. 45's trolley is tied down clear of the overhead wire
Ian Yearsley

All in all, the TMS has much to be proud of as it reaches its 50 years jubilee. The passion for trams that drove people of my generation to create the TMS came from seeing them in our towns and cities, later generations are showing similar enthusiasm through having seen them in action at the Museum. There are signs that future generations may have the same enthusiasm, though based on a broader interest in the tramway as a part of social and industrial history. Southampton car 45 has already seen more years in preservation ownership than it did in its home city. If the future seems difficult, it is worth remembering that the TMS now owns its own premises, has all its cars under cover, and is debt-free. Such things seemed like a dream in its first year, 1955-56, when it had a collection of debts and notices to quit, yet had the vision of that first bold purchase in 1948, when Southampton 45 was bought for £10.

Leeds tower wagon 2 follows Prague 180 at the bookshop unloading point. The works car has a trolley pole at one end and a bow collector at the other. Overhead wiring at the NTM has to accommodate fixed and swivel head trolleys, pantographs and bow collectors.

Ian Yearsley

Presidents of the TMS

Chaceley Humpidge (later the Revd.) was the first president of the Society, from 1958 to his death in 1972. In 1964-65 he was also president of the Municipal Passenger Transport Association and in 1967 he was also president of the Omnibus Society. After 1972 there was no TMS president until 1981 when the office was revived on an annual basis, but in the mid-1970s four vice-presidents were appointed: Major Charles Walker, George Hearse, Merlyn Bacon and Basil Miller, and were followed by Graham Mather, Geoffrey Hyde, Geoffrey Claydon and David Senior.

Presidents from 1981 onwards were: Richard Fairbairn 1981-82, Doug Vernon 1982-83, Roger Mercer 1983-84, Maurice O'Connor 1984-85, Geoffrey Hyde 1985-86, John Price 1986-87, Derek Shepherd 1987-88, Mrs Marjorie Hartwell 1988-89, Ian Stewart 1989-90, Jim Soper 1990-91, Harry Barnett 1991-92, John Brooke 1992-93, Laurence Dutton 1993-94, Tommy Thompson 1994-95, Alan Bertram 1995-96, Brian Pickup 1996-97, Ian Dougill 1997-98, Richard Wiseman 1998-99, Mrs Ann Marshall 1999-2000, Mike Crabtree 2000-01, Sir Neil Cossons OBE 2001-02, Roger Webster 2002-03, Keith Chadbourne 2003-04, Derek Redmond 2004-05 and Geoffrey Claydon CB 2005-06.

Members of the Board of Management for 2004-05

Back row, left to right: Bob Pennyfather, Kyle Hulme, Karen Rigg, Roger Webster, Derek Redmond (President 2004-5), Malcolm Wright, Andrew Willis, James Blythe (Minutes Secretary), David Frodsham.

Front row: David Senior (Vice-President), Winstan Bond (Treasurer), Colin Heaton (Chairman), Ian Dougill (Secretary), Geoffrey Claydon (Vice-President, President elect 2005-6). **Glynn Wilton**

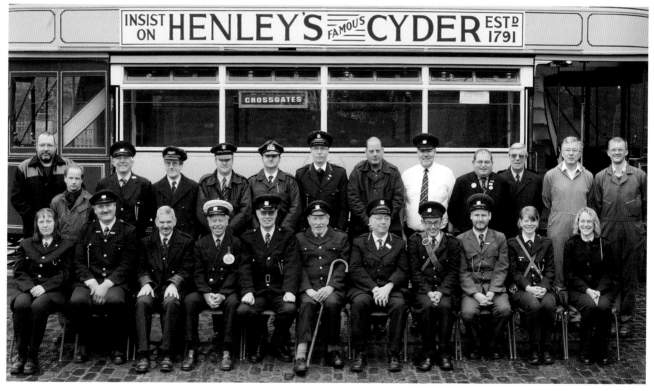

The Tram Crews

No history of either the Museum or the Society would be complete without due reference to the people who make so much possible, day after day, week after week - the members who serve as tram crews, undertake engineering tasks in the Workshop, act as Museum Guides, and undertake many other, often menial, important tasks. The group pictured here represents a far greater number of regular volunteers. **David Muscroft**

By early 2005 the restoration of Leeds 345 had progressed well. The car stands on the depot headshunt on one of its early forays into the world outside the Workshop.

Aaron Johansson

Gala night atmosphere on a President's Evening as Blackpool 40 and London 1622 await members and their guests. There is always something special about travelling at night on the Museum tramway.

Ian Yearsley

The interest in trams transcends differences in age and seniority. And the interior of 1622, with many distinctive London features, provides plenty to talk about.

Ian Yearsley

TMS members' first-hand memories are an important historical resource; as part of a 'living history' presentation, Laurence Dutton here shares memories of Leeds with an attentive audience.

Ian Yearsley

Opening of the restaurant in the Red Lion has given a whole new style to party events such as this President's Evening. Eating a meal with a view of tramcar tops passing the windows is an experience to savour.

Ian Yearsley

A motorist's eye view of the Museum tramway from the Matlock road. Tram crews have reported seeing drivers pull up sharply and even get out of their cars in disbelief on seeing a tram moving along the hillside above them.

Ian Yearsley

Liverpool 869 newly repainted in June 2001, in front of the Exhibition Hall which incorporates arched window castings from Doncaster's 1902 tram depot.

Mike Crabtree

Members assemble in Mrs Poplar's garden in August 1965 for Merlyn and Faith Bacon's Silver Wedding anniversary. Mrs Gladys Poplar is on the right on the front row. The house, now TMS property, was named after her.

Mike Crabtree

Paisley 68 runs to the depot at the end of a summer's day. Is this really a museum, or have we stepped back into the 1920s? The balustrade on the Library roof stands out against the sky.

Ian Yearsley

Mrs Gwynneth Dunwoody, M.P., chairman of the Transport Select Committee, tries out the lift on Berlin 3006, the first AccessTram, watched by Amber Valley M.P. Judy Mallaber and (on the car) Geoffrey Claydon. Chief Driving Instructor David Tudor operates the lift.

Mike Crabtree

Oporto 273 made a demonstration run for TMS Board members and others shortly after it arrived in June 1996, and before its extensive restoration in the Workshop.

Mike Crabtree

Re-enacting the original 1959 inspection of the Museum site, diesel locomotive 'GMJ' otherwise 'Ted' hauls Sheffield 15 in September 1999. Behind it are Leeds 399 and Newcastle 102.

Mike Crabtree

Sunderland 100 (otherwise MET 331) in its British Steel advertising livery at the Gateshead Garden Festival, alongside Newcastle 102 in a more recognisable local colour scheme.
Mike Crabtree

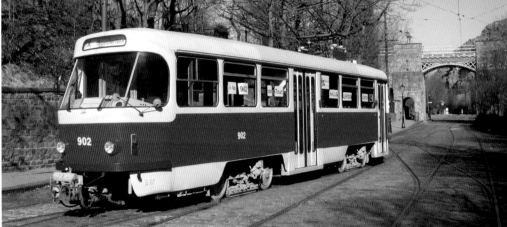

Halle 902, newly arrived at the Museum, stands at the Depot entrance. This car is destined to be fitted with a wheelchair lift to become the second AccessTram.
Aaron Johansson

Author's afterword

The credit for the achievements recorded in this book should go to the members of the Tramway Museum Society, together with their Board and its officers and employees. Opinions expressed and any errors which may be found are my own. My involvement with tramway preservation goes back to 1948 and I joined the TMS in its first year; my first visit to the Crich site was in 1959, and I have been involved in its development ever since, most of all during the mid-1990s when I was employed on a part-time basis at the Museum to compile an index to the trade journals in the Library.

Most of the material in this book is taken from TMS annual reports, journals, Contact and earlier newsletters; in addition I have consulted with many people. I am particularly grateful to John Barrie, Winstan Bond, Richard Clarke, Geoffrey Claydon, Mike Crabtree, Dennis Gill, George Hearse, Colin Heaton, David Holt, Geoffrey Hyde, Aaron, Jonathan and Peter Johansson, Ian Musgrove, John Price, Alan Ralphs, Val Ross, Ian Rowson, David Senior, John Senior, Derek Shepherd, John Slater, Rosy Thacker, Peter Waller, Fred Ward, Glynn Wilton, Malcolm Wright and Lesley Wyld for help in many different ways. Material has also been included and updated from the 1998 booklet 'Tramway Adventure' which celebrated 50 years of tramcar preservation, and from an earlier TMS publication 'Ten Years at Crich'.

This does not pretend to be a full history, either of the Society or its Museum. There remains a great deal that could be written, whether on the development of a tramway, the changing dynamics of a voluntary society, the business history of a seemingly impossible enterprise, or on personalities and anecdotes. If this book encourages all or any of these to be written, I shall be delighted. Meanwhile, there is fresh history to be made as well as recorded at the Museum; come and take part!

Ian Yearsley, Putney and South Wingfield, 2005

Tramway Museum Story
2005-2015

by Paul Abell & Lynn Wagstaff

Updated aims & objectives

The principal objectives of the Tramway Museum Society are:

- To maintain for the benefit of the Nation an operating tramway museum.

- To promote the permanent preservation of tramway vehicles and equipment, and items of general transport interest (either historic, scientific or educational) and to work as necessary with other institutions, societies and bodies, having similar aims, in any part of the world.

- To promote and further the study of and research into tramways and other forms of transport.

If they had not been to Crich for ten years, a visitor passing through the village in 2015 might well look around them and feel that little had changed. Approaching the Museum, however, they might notice quieter roads and less dust and, making their way along the access road to the car park, they could be surprised not to meet lorries coming and going – this has become the norm since the quarry was 'mothballed' in July 2010.

The visitor would surely notice the new admissions building, completed in 2007. In 2014 its appearance was modified to resemble an Edwardian ticket office/waiting room. Its colourful exterior - complete with "stained-glass" windows - and redesigned interior offer a much warmer welcome to new arrivals. Inside is a small display of items for sale, intended to attract visitors as, hopefully some hours later, they leave the Museum.

Admissions Building with updated appearance.
National Tramway Museum

Victoria Park is one of the first views our visitors have of the Museum. The bandstand area has seen piecemeal improvements over the years, with the addition of paving at the rail side northbound and the Ashton shelter for the tram stop, but this was only the beginning…

Victoria Park and Bandstand with landscaping, railings and paving.
National Tramway Museum

To coincide with the 100th anniversary of the bandstand from Stretford, Phase 1 of the project north of the Bowes-Lyon bridge to create a 1930s environment was implemented over the winter of 2011-12. Funding for the improvements at Victoria Park came from the Subscriber Plus Fund, into which TMS members contribute to fund improvements purely for the benefit of visitors. Improvements entailed landscaping the area around the bandstand to create a grassed park area with bench seats and pathways. The park was enclosed by a dwarf wall of stonework, on which were erected wrought iron railings from former school premises in Leeds, along with paving around the west and north perimeter of the park. To complete the work an appropriate piece of street furniture in the shape of a bollard from Leeds was placed to prevent vehicular traffic mounting the corner of the paving. Finally, members of the Leeds Transport Historical Society prepared and painted the bandstand itself; then, in July 2012 and with local bands playing, the Mayor of Trafford and the Mayor of Amber Valley jointly opened the newly created Park.

Indoor Play Area 2014.
National Tramway Museum

Walking towards Town End, visitors with young children will discover improvements to the Indoor Play Area, which was refurbished in 2014. New flooring has been fitted, the walls have been painted and, most importantly, colourful new tramcar-themed play equipment has been installed, together with seating for adults waiting for their charges to use up surplus energy.

Other visitors might pass on directly to the Exhibition Hall, but most will probably fail to notice a significant change, adopted in the interests of both economy and the environment – the westward-facing roof of this building has been fitted with solar panels.

Within, however, the changes are evident to all.

Funding totalling £500,000 from the Derbyshire Economic Partnership and the Wolfson Foundation enabled a complete redesign of the displays in the Exhibition Hall to be undertaken in 2009. The result was the Century of Trams exhibition, opened in June 2010, which makes use of a wide cross-section of the Society's collections to illustrate the development of tramways in Britain in the 100 years from 1860 to 1960. The new exhibition also makes better use of the available space in the Exhibition Hall to give visitors a display with the 'wow factor'.

The display was enhanced in February 2014 by the addition of the 1892 South Staffordshire Tramways Fox-type pressed-steel Electric Construction Corporation truck, on loan from the Science Museum, and a Birmingham Corporation Tramways EMB 'Burnley' bogie, on loan from Birmingham City Museums, joining the Museum collection's own 1895 Snaefell Milnes bogie from the Isle of Man.

Century of Trams exhibition, opened June 2010.
National Tramway Museum

Stone Workshop restoration 2011

A little further down the street, the historic Stone Workshop, dating back to the days of George Stephenson and the development of the quarry in the 1840s, has benefitted from a restoration, assisted considerably by £893,500 from the Heritage Lottery Fund. Work began in 2010, but was interrupted by the severe winter weather of 2010-2011. The project has provided additional exhibition space on the reinstated first floor of the workshop, which has been fitted out as a new Exhibition and Discovery Centre. The first floor is linked by a footbridge to the Conservation Workshop's Viewing Gallery, while the ground floor is now the Stephenson Learning Centre, particularly useful for accommodating school parties.

The completed building was opened to the public by the leader of Derbyshire County Council, Councillor Andrew Lewer, on 20 July 2011. In the same year the George Stephenson Discovery Centre won the Derbyshire Heritage Award for Best Exhibition.

Left: The New Exhibition.

Right: Opening of the exhibition: Dianne Jeffrey, a member of the East Midlands Committee of the Heritage Lottery Fund; Colin Heaton, Chairman of the TMS; Councillor Andrew Lewer, Leader of Derbyshire County Council.

National Tramway Museum

Assembly Rooms exhibitions.

*Left to right :
Survive and Thrive:
the Electric Era,
Making of Crich,
Tramway Tommies
and Clippie girls.*

**National Tramway
Museum**

Within the Assembly Rooms building, completely new exhibitions can be seen. In one half of the space, *Survive & Thrive: the Electric Era,* which opened in October 2012, examines the introduction of modern tramway systems in cities throughout the UK.

The other half of the Assembly Rooms building has been redesignated a temporary exhibition area. Opened in 2014, it first housed the *Making of Crich* exhibition. At the beginning of the 2015 season this was replaced by *Tramway Tommies and Clippie Girls,* which tells of the effect of the First World War on Britain's tramways and tramwaymen – and women. One of the themes of this exhibition, the recruitment of tramway staff, was carried beyond the indoor exhibition space with the transformation of Chesterfield 7 into a recruitment tram. This specially-decorated tramcar, sporting banners originally used on a variety of recruiting cars, could be seen running throughout the 2015 season.

*Town End shelter
during refurbishment
2014.*
Malcolm Wright

Moving on to Town End Terminus, the visitor might notice the new Pram and Buggy Shelter, and their attention will certainly be drawn to the Birmingham Tram Shelter, restored in 2014. The Police Box, also, was repainted in 2013/14. This was not as simple a project as it may sound. The Box is Grade II listed, and the paint colour had to match exactly that of the Police pillar behind the Depot gates, and that of paint samples taken from the Police Box itself.

New tram stop at Glory Mine 2014.
National Tramway Museum

A tram ride from Town End will reveal the views over the Derwent Valley to be unchanged, as would be expected, but the passenger might be surprised to see other visitors seated at wooden picnic tables on the bank above as the tram approaches Glory Mine. This new picnic site can be accessed from the Glory Mine stop, which has been redesigned as a passenger-friendly area. Visitors also have the opportunity to take a country walk to Crich Stand, the Sherwood Foresters' Memorial Tower.

Site of former lead smelter.
National Tramway Museum

Returning to Wakebridge and along the Woodland Walk, the last of our major changes can be seen – the Lead Smelter site. This rare survival can be viewed from a specially-designed wooden walkway, and an interpretative panel stands nearby. The work was funded by the Association for Industrial Archaeology; the grant was made in 2012, but for various reasons the project did not get under way until 2014. The Lead Smelter was opened for public viewing in 2015, giving an insight into what was once an extremely important local industry which can trace its history back to Roman times.

Preparations for renewing trackwork at town end 2009/10.
National Tramway Museum

Left: Initial preparations at Town End 2009/10.
National Tramway Museum

Centre: Preparation for new track work at Bowes-Lyon bridge interlaced track 2014/15.
National Tramway Museum

Right: Sealing setts at Bowes-Lyon bridge interlaced track with bitumen , 2014/15.
MikeCrabtree

Other improvements are more subtle, but will no doubt be noticed by dedicated tram enthusiasts. The use of a long handle rather than the traditional point-iron to change the points into the second track at Town End is the most obvious indication that this end of the demonstration tramway track has been completely relaid. This project was undertaken during the winter of 2009-10. It was found most cost-effective to use modern-style pointwork and Ri60 rail, which is slightly deeper than the 35G rail previously used for relaying the loop at Wakebridge; it was chosen so that the area can be paved with setts at a future date. Meanwhile, the relaying of the Wakebridge loop halfway up the line has been accomplished with very little change to the essential ambience of the area. The whole of the line from Wakebridge up to Glory Mine had been relaid in either Ri60 or 35G rail by 2012, while the interlaced track under the Bowes-Lyon Bridge and the setts were relaid during the winter of 2014-15.

The trams themselves are in a number of ways the most difficult of our exhibits both to house and to maintain, yet the experience of a ride on a traditional tramcar is an essential part of the Museum's appeal to visitors. Enjoyable as this may be, it is important to remember that there are many other parts of the Museum which have to be maintained and developed, even when they are much less in the public eye.

The continued operation of a number of vintage tramcars in the 21st Century reflects great credit on the skills of the Engineering Team. Their ingenuity makes it possible for participants on internet forums to argue about which tram should be made operational next, rather than whether it is going to be possible to enjoy a ride at all.

The essential part played by the Museum's engineers and craftspeople in keeping a selection of tramcars available for demonstration has been complemented by their efforts in completing a succession of major restorations which have added significantly to the Museum's exhibits. The transformation of Leeds 345 from a dusty relic in the store at Clay Cross into an immaculate operating tramcar was followed by the restoration of Cardiff 131, while perhaps the most spectacular addition to the operational fleet in recent years has been London United Tramways 159.

The replacement of the traditional tramcar fleet at Blackpool has resulted in the addition of four more trams for visitors to see at Crich, one as a static exhibit in the Exhibition Hall, two as very useful members of the operational fleet, and one whose modern control gear has challenged our Workshop staff.

Maintenance of the existing fleet by its nature tends to be taken for granted; perhaps unfairly the newcomers attract more attention, but it was ever thus...

Installation of new track work at Bowes-Lyon bridge interlaced track prior to concrete pour 2014/15.
Malcolm Wright

Nevertheless, let us look in more detail at the trams our engineers have returned to operation or prepared for display during the past 10 years, together with others which have been recently added to the fleet or to our stock of future restoration projects.

Restoration projects 2005 - 2015

Left: Leeds 345 during restoration 2005.

National Tramway Museum

Right: Leeds 345 upper and lower saloons reunited.

National Tramway Museum

Leeds 345

The launch of Leeds 345 as an operational tram in April 2006 represented the culmination of almost half a century's endeavour by the Leeds Transport Historical Society, which had first secured the tram for preservation when Leeds City Tramways (LCT) ceased operations in 1959, and also reflected the help given by the Tramcar Sponsorship Organisation in funding the restoration of the car.

Originally built by Leeds City Tramways at their Kirkstall Road Works as an open-balcony tram in 1921, 345 was one of 34 such cars rebuilt as totally-enclosed cars in the late 1930s. The rebuild was undertaken partly as a modernisation programme to reflect changes in tramcar design and passenger expectations, and partly because Leeds could not afford to buy any more new trams at the time. Withdrawn from service in 1948, the car was used as a store in Swinegate depot until the closure of the tramways, after which it arrived at Crich in December 1959.

Not being a serviceable tramcar, 345 was a low priority for attention at the time, and it was transferred to the store at Clay Cross in February 1982. Having fortunately survived the fire of 1999, it was eventually selected for restoration, as it was more or less complete. Extraction from Clay Cross followed and a very thorough programme of work began in 2003.

The restoration of 345 gained an international element in April 2006 when TMS Chairman Colin Heaton and member Dai Hawkins presented a paper on the project at the annual meeting of AHN (Arbeitsgemainschaft Historischer Nahverkehr - the German Association of Local Transport Collections) in Rostock. In addition the tram was judged to be the Best Self-Propelled Vehicle in the Heritage Railway Association's 2006 Carriage & Wagon Competition.

Cardiff 131 returns from Clay Cross, August 2007.

National Tramway Museum

Cardiff 131

Cardiff 131 was the first tram to arrive at Crich, in May 1959, but the survival of this water car after the closure of the Cardiff City Tramways in 1950 was purely a matter of chance. A group of enthusiasts enquired about the possibility of buying one of Cardiff's trams for preservation. They had all been sold for scrap, but 131 had been overlooked when the disposal of trams had been arranged. Before the Museum at Crich was established in 1959 the difficulty of housing preserved trams was the most serious obstacle to their survival, and sadly a few trams were lost to us for lack of somewhere secure to keep them. 131, however, had the advantage of being relatively small, so that storage could be arranged for it in Cardiff and, later, Gloucester before its transfer to Crich.

Some work was done on 131 in the 1960s but, as it was clearly not going to be suitable for carrying visitors, it entered a long period of storage, first at Crich, then at Clay Cross from 1971. Happily the Tramcar Sponsorship Organisation was able to fund its restoration (one of many projects for which the TSO has provided essential funding), while the Transport Trust contributed £2,000 in the form of its 2008 Peter Allen Award. The tram was returned from Clay Cross to Crich on 31st

Cardiff 131 with our Patron driving, May 2009.

National Tramway Museum

August 2007, and its restoration was completed by the Workshop staff in time for the tram to appear as an operational vehicle in the celebrations of 50 Years at Crich in 2009. A fitting ceremony on 20th May 2009 brought together TMS Patron HRH the Duke of Gloucester and Deputy Lord Mayor of Cardiff Councillor Keith Hyde as the tram, in a recreation of its 1959 arrival, was once again transported into the Museum premises and unloaded. After unloading, however, it was driven on this occasion by the Duke.

At the Museum 131 is primarily a works car, rather than for carrying passengers, and performs an important function, cleaning our tracks. On occasion it has been used for the Ultimate Tram Driving Experience.

Amazingly November 2011 found the grinding function of 131 put to good use once more on the very exposed New South Promenade section of the modernised Blackpool tramway, north of Starr Gate. The tram spent some time cleaning off the deposits which had accumulated on the rails during the period between the track being laid and the reopening of the tramway. Since the reopening, of course, the regular passage of trams has shined the rails automatically.

In addition 131 visited Beamish in April 2010 for the *Power From The Past* event, but it has not yet returned to Wales, partly because there is no line in Wales on which it could be put through its paces. This is a shame, as it is the only operational preserved Welsh electric tramcar.

London United Tramways 159 at Wakebridge.
National Tramway Museum

LUT 159

London United Tramways 159, the next tram to be completed by the workshop, represents a much more ambitious restoration. Built for London United Tramways in

1902, car 159 had been surplus to requirements almost as soon as it was delivered. Many of the grandiose schemes of the LUT had come to nothing and the Company found itself with many more trams than it needed.

Withdrawal from service and sale came in 1923, a time when planning rules were not as strict as they are today, and 159 became one of three tram bodies serving as a bungalow in Ewhurst Green, near Cranleigh in Surrey. Discovered by members of the London County Council Tramways Trust (LCCTT) in 1978, it was acquired as a long-term restoration project, and finally took its place in the Workshop in 2005. In this case the cost of the work was met by the LCCTT, which does not confine its attentions to trams from the former London County Council.

London United Tramways 159 during restoration.
National Tramway Museum

Restoration proved to be a protracted affair, with a number of interesting experiences along the way. The LUT cars were built to a high-quality specification, and the saloon has been fitted out with the luxurious finishings of 1902 – other tramways used such large trams as workmen's cars, but this was definitely not the case with the LUT. The Robinson staircases at each end are of a special design with two straight sections linked by a small landing half-way up. 159 is the only tram in the Crich collection to demonstrate this feature.

Providing a pair of the appropriate Brill 22E bogies for the tram was planned to be a matter of regauging a pair of bogies acquired from Lisbon for the purpose. However their condition made it necessary to have four new sideframes cast. The launch of the tramcar was affected by some teething problems with weight transfer, which resulted in a minor derailment. Naturally this was followed by suitable remedial action in the Workshop and the tram is now a very reliable and elegant performer, much in demand on fine days.

London County Council 1 is another project funded by the LCCTT. It is not only a tram originating from LCC Tramways but also an exceptional vehicle which was built as the prototype for a fleet intended to take passengers through the 1930s in comfort. LCC 1's advanced styling was matched by a number of advances in tramcar construction, and the tram's restoration is being fully documented to ensure that no detail of its revolutionary design goes unrecorded.

The gradual restoration of this tram is going to be a sight to see for some years to come, but LCC 1 will be beautiful when it is completed. The original blue livery, surviving under the subsequent layers of red, is suspiciously close in shade to the blue of LUT 159, but there could hardly be a greater contrast than the two trams.

Blackpool 298, now at Clay Cross.
National Tramway Museum

Blackpool 298

Blackpool Corporation Brush car 298, withdrawn from service in 1976, was selected for preservation despite its poor condition because it retained more original body features than any other surviving tramcar of its class. The restoration process however was challenging and prolonged, with available funding being insufficient for completion.

In 2004 the Board of Management agreed that 298, then housed at the former Manchester Ship Canal Railway Workshops ('Mode Wheel') near Eccles, should be moved to Crich. Health and Safety concerns had to be addressed before the tramcar could be prepared for transfer.

As well as the tramcar itself, a large amount of unfinished work and spare parts had to be transported. Gathering these together with the intention of crating them up and loading them into 298's saloon, the team also found spares belonging to other vehicles as well as tools and other miscellaneous items. It was decided to transport all the material, sort it at Crich, and move the surplus on to Clay Cross.

Even getting 298 out of Unit F, where it was stored, proved problematic. Bulky pieces of equipment had to be moved out of the way first, and changes to the workshop complex meant that it was impossible to get a heavy haulage vehicle to the shed door. Nevertheless, the TMS team, in consultation with Scott's Heavy Haulage, arrived at a solution.

On the morning of Monday 26th September 2005, Scott's heavy-duty forklift truck removed the wood machining centre and band saw which were blocking the exit, and then prepared to move 298 outside for the first time in perhaps 20 years.

It was dusk by the time 298 - shrouded now in tarpaulins as it was not weathertight - on Scott's big rig, followed by the support lorry, trailer and forklift, emerged onto the road. Crich was reached very late in the evening, and the following morning 298 was unloaded and moved into the depot. Some restoration work was done, but for reasons of space, the decision was taken to move it to the Museum's Clay Cross premises in 2014, where it has been surveyed with a view to a future more extensive restoration.

Edinburgh 35 prior to conservation work 2013.

Mike Crabtree

Edinburgh 35

Edinburgh 35 came to Crich in 1989, since when it has functioned as a static exhibit.

35 remained the property of Edinburgh City Council until May 2008 when, after many years of negotiation conducted by TMS Secretary Ian Dougill, the Council agreed to transfer the ownership of the tramcar to the TMS.

Conservation work was carried out on 35 in 2013, in preparation for its inclusion in the Century of Trams exhibition. When the advertisements for British Gas, which had been in place on the upper deck panels since 1988, were removed, two original hand painted adverts were found beneath. These can now be seen on the tramcar as it stands in the Exhibition Hall.

Mike Crabtree, Chairman of the Tramcar Sponsorship Organisation, presents a cheque to TMS Chairman, Colin Heaton for conservation of Sheffield 510.
National Tramway Museum

Sheffield 510

The relaunch of the overhauled, repaired and renovated Sheffield 510 in May 2014 marked the end of almost two years of painstaking effort by Workshop staff, contractors and members of the Tramcar Sponsorship Organisation, which, along with a generous private donation, sponsored the project.

Work began in August 2012, with an overhaul of the seating and the removal of the trolley pole. In the following month the tram was lifted off its truck. When the truck was thoroughly examined, badly worn pinions and road gears were found, providing an explanation for the excessive gear noise which had been noticed in the tram's latter days of operation. The truck was then dismantled; each component was inspected, repaired and painted, with many replacement pins, bolts and bushes having to be manufactured.

During the examination and dismantling process, corrosion on an axle, caused by water leaking under the wheel seats, was found. Great efforts were made to achieve the restoration of the resilient drive, an innovative and distinctive feature of Sheffield's Roberts cars and the reason for the tram's practically noiseless running.

Upper and lower deck exterior panels were taken off; the lower deck panels were to be repainted, while the upper, featuring murals depicting tramcars from Sheffield's history, were to be removed for conservation. Replicas of these murals would adorn the replacement panels. Visitors watching the work in progress from the Workshop Viewing Gallery might have been alarmed to see the lower deck panels being painted a vivid pink; this colour however was used because it is particularly good for revealing surface imperfections, enabling the Museum's coach painters to prepare a perfect canvas to receive the tram's new blue and cream 'Last Tram' livery.

Sheffield 510 after completion of overhaul and repainting 2014.
National Tramway Museum

Another major element of the restoration was that of the tram's wiring. Both upper and lower saloons were completely rewired, and all light fittings were cleaned. Finally the tram was lifted back onto its truck and its trolley pole refitted, and it re-entered service as part of the 2014 Best of Sheffield event. On their website, the TSO thanked the many staff and volunteers at Crich who had put 'an exceptional amount of hours and commitment into 510'.

LCC 106

LCC 106, first restored in 1983 after its arrival at Crich and frequently used for demonstration since then, was taken into the Workshop in 2013 for an extensive overhaul, again sponsored by the LCCTT. The process was begun by lifting the body of 106 from its truck and placing it on a body truck; thus the tramcar entered the workshop in two sections, which could be worked on both at once. It would be a full year before the two halves were reunited.

Yet another year saw 106 out on the track again, as tests and driver re-familiarisation were carried out in preparation for the tramcar's return to operation. This took place during the *Classic London* event of June 2015. Leon Daniels, Surface Transport Director at Transport for London, officially handed 106 over to Crich's Traffic Department and, together with TMS Chairman Colin Heaton and LCCTT Chairman Ian Ross, launched the restored tram, thus beginning the next phase of its long and useful life.

Blackpool Arrivals

At the end of traditional tramcar operation in Blackpool in November 2011, and the subsequent modernisation of the line to Fleetwood, a question arose: which trams from the traditional fleet should come to the Museum? This in turn raised storage problems potentially as acute as when Blackpool had offered the TMS the earlier set of cars nearly 40 years previously, but nevertheless, four of the old fleet have made a significant addition to the Museum collection.

Blackpool 'Balloon' 249

The first of these to arrive at Crich was Blackpool 'Balloon' 249. Latterly numbered 712, this was built as an open-topper, delivered to Blackpool by English Electric in 1934 as part of the great modernisation of the tramway at that time. It was given a top-cover in 1941-42 to cope with the influx of winter traffic brought by the many wartime training camps around Blackpool. The tram arrived at Crich in 2010 after it had been repainted at Blackpool in 1930s livery to represent the period in the Century of Trams exhibition.

*Blackpool 249 (712)
prior to installation in
the Century of Trams
exhibition 2010.*
Dan Heeley

*Blackpool 630 enters
service in 2012.*
Malcolm Wright

Blackpool 630

Built by Brush at Loughborough in 1937, Blackpool 630 was one of 20 high-quality cars (the Brush development of the previous English Electric Railcoaches) which were the mainstay of year-round services along the Blackpool-Fleetwood route for many years. It was numbered 293 until the entire Blackpool fleet was renumbered in 1968, when it became 630. Delivered to Crich in December 2011, it entered service on 12th May 2012, as part of a special event featuring vehicles built by the Brush Company.

Blackpool 236

Blackpool 236, universally known as a 'boat' though more formally designated a 'luxury toastrack', was delivered to Blackpool by English Electric in 1934 as an early contribution to the modernisation of Blackpool Corporation Tramways in the 1930s. With funding from the TMS and the TSO, 236 was overhauled by Blackpool Transport Services Ltd and repainted in the style of the 1950s before it was transported to the Museum, where it commenced operation on 3rd June 2012. It has since been fitted with the traditional four festoons of coloured lights down from the trolley tower.

Blackpool 762

Blackpool 762 was the last standard-gauge double-deck tramcar built for service on a commercial British tramway - at least until now, and for the foreseeable future. It entered service in Blackpool in 1982 as a development of the previous front-entrance double-decker (car 761, built in 1979) with a second doorway on each side. It arrived at Crich in

November 2011.

The tram has a number of features which set it apart from the other operational trams at the Museum, not least its Westinghouse chopper control, and commissioning it was a particularly tricky job, but it finally became operational on 13 September 2014, as part of the Museum's Electric 50 event.

Nottingham 166

The Museum was fortunate to receive the four Blackpool trams as complete vehicles; currently the lower saloon body of Nottingham 166 represents an acquisition at the other end of the scale, but it is an extremely important one - a representative of the tram fleet of a large city close to the Museum, and the largest tramway operator in the East Midlands.

166's lower saloon was sold to become a dwelling in Lincolnshire, and in March 2007 it was transported to the Clay Cross store for eventual restoration.

Left: Lower deck of Nottingham 166 in Lincolnshire.

National Tramway Museum

Right: Nottingham 166 on its journey to Clay Cross, 2007.

National Tramway Museum

Gateshead 52 loaded at Clay Cross for transfer to Beamish Museum

National Tramway Museum

Gateshead 52

One tram has left the Museum collection: Gateshead 52 was permanently transferred to Beamish, The Living History Museum of the North in 2013, and arrived in the North East in January 2014.

Blackpool and Fleetwood 40 operating in Blackpool, 2010.

Malcolm Wright

Vehicle loans 2005 - 2015

In addition to the trams owned by the TMS, vehicles loaned from elsewhere have been used to supplement our exhibitions and demonstration fleet.

Brush-built 1886 Cardiff horse tram 21 has been on loan to the Museum from the National Museum of Wales since 2009, while 1897 Milnes–built Leeds horse tram 107 has been static at the Museum since September 2013, following its restoration by the Leeds Transport Historical Society.

Two works vehicles from the Tramlink network operated around Croydon by Transport for London were unusual arrivals at Crich in January 2010. Both vehicles were built in

Germany by Sollinger Hütte for Deutsche Bahn; 058 is a diesel-propelled four-wheeled unit fitted with a hydraulic crane, and 061 is a matching flat trailer. They have proved to be very useful additions to the works fleet at the Museum.

One of the features of the last ten years has been the explosion in trams being transported around the country from museum to museum, often as visiting attractions for special events. It has to be remembered that trams are bulky, awkward loads to transport, especially double-deckers. Great care must be taken when loading and unloading such precious artefacts, and even after routes have been planned meticulously there is always the chance of something going wrong.

Such is the range of the collection at Crich that we can run many excellent events with our resident tramcars. Nevertheless both our events and those at other locations have been enriched by a number of loans in recent years, in which the expertise of Scott's Heavy Haulage has been invaluable.

2009 saw Beyer Peacock steam tram 47 (for many years Works Shunter No. 2 at the Gorton plant of BP) return to its native Manchester for an event at the Museum of Science & Industry commemorating the building of the first Garratt loco by Beyer Peacock.

The hazards inherent in moving double-deck tramcars were demonstrated in 2010 when an overhanging tree damaged Johannesburg 60 soon after it had left the Museum to take part in Blackpool Tramway's 125th anniversary celebrations. In the circumstances it was felt prudent to restrict the participation of TMS cars in the festivities to single-deckers that could be transported with much less chance of incident. Blackpool & Fleetwood 2 was a very appropriate substitute, dating as it does from the first days of the Blackpool & Fleetwood Tramroad in 1898, and it was given the honour of leading the cavalcade of historic Blackpool tramcars at the event. In contrast a seized traction motor armature bearing suffered by Blackpool 167 while visiting Blackpool once more demonstrated the potential difficulties of operating vintage vehicles despite the most careful attention.

Grimsby & Immingham 14 on display at Immingham Dock , July 2012.
National Tramway Museum

One of the least likely trams to go on tour was probably Grimsby & Immingham 14. Loaned to Immingham Town Museum, 14 was put on static display at Immingham Dock over the weekend of 21st-22nd July 2012. The tram's visit formed part of the Centenary celebrations of the opening of the Dock, then under the ownership of the Great Central Railway, by King George V.

*Glasgow 1068
arrives at Beamish
Museum on loan,
2014.*

Alison Bailey

Paisley 68 was repainted in blue route livery as Glasgow 1068 in 2012 for the 50th Anniversary of the closure of Glasgow Corporation Tramways, thanks to funding from the Scottish Tramway & Transport Society, and subsequently operated at Beamish Museum the following spring. Blackpool 167 followed it to Beamish for a visit in spring 2014.

*Chesterfield 8
on display in
Chesterfield,
May 2013.*

**National Tramway
Museum**

2013 saw two more trams go on their travels for static display: Chesterfield horse car 8 returned to Chesterfield in May as part of the Chesterfield Arts Festival, while Southampton 45 visited Kimberley in June during Centenary celebrations for the Nottinghamshire & Derbyshire Tramway.

1914-built Blackpool & Fleetwood 'Box' 40, for many years the subject of a long-term loan to Blackpool, was overhauled in 2013/14 a project funded by the TMS, Blackpool Transport Services and the Fylde Tramway Society. The work was jointly carried out by the Museum and Blackpool Transport Services Ltd in preparation for the car's centenary and the Electric 50 event commemorating 50 years of electric tramcar operation at Crich. The project was kindly supported by the Fylde Tramway Society, Dorlec, Scotts Heavy Haulage,

Left: Blackpool & Fleetwood 'Box' 40 seen here at Blackpool returned to Crich for four months in 2014.

National Tramway Museum

Mike Crabtree presents Colin Heaton the controller key for the loaned Blackpool 711 during 2014.

National Tramway Museum

Friends of 40, the TMS and BTS. The celebrations included the car returning to Crich in July 2014.

A very different Blackpool tram arrived at the Museum on 9th April 2014, Blackpool 711 being part of a temporary exchange for 167. Originally a sister car to 249 in the Exhibition Hall, 711 was retained by Blackpool Transport Services after the end of traditional tramway operation in Blackpool and modernised with widened doors and a number of safety features to enable it to supplement the new Bombardier Flexity trams on the upgraded line. Painted in a purple livery to match the Bombardier trams, it was a striking sight at Crich. 711 returned to Blackpool together with Blackpool & Fleetwood 40 on 29th October, while 167 returned to Crich on 29th August after a successful visit to Blackpool.

Newcastle 114 arrives on loan from Beamish Museum.

National Tramway Museum

The *Electric 50* celebrations in September 2014 also saw a short visit to Crich by Newcastle 114, a short-canopy open-top four-wheeler, from Beamish Museum. 114 is the only operating example in Britain of this type of electric tram, which is not represented in the Crich collection. This was a significant milestone, being the first time the Museum had operated an electric tram from another heritage tramway.

Over the last ten years much work has been necessary in replacing infrastructure such as the track, as described earlier. This had typically been acquired secondhand from closed tramways in the 1960s and is now, naturally, approaching the end of its serviceable life.

Meanwhile the task of keeping the tramway in operation has to work within the bounds of contemporary regulations. Listing the entire host of individual measures would be tedious in the extreme, but to give an example, the projects to relay the track at Town End and on the interlace turned the area into a CDM site in accordance with the Construction (Design & Management) Regulations 2007, with access prohibited to all but authorised persons. Another example is the tower wagons used for more than a century to gain access to the overhead wires, which have now become Mobile Elevated Works Platforms (MEWPs), subject to the requirements of the Work at Height Regulations and the Lifting Equipment & Lifting Operations Regulations 1998, which prompted the rebodying of Tower Wagon 3 as Tower Wagon 4.

The Health & Safety Committee meets regularly to consider such changes, and to review circumstances and incidents with health and safety implications, while the Museum is represented on the Light Rail Engineers Group and the HMRI Tramway Standards Verification Group, among other bodies.

Actual work on the infrastructure becomes obvious from time to time by virtue of the inevitable disruption which such construction projects cause to the life of the Museum; and of course such work may involve changes to more than just the track. For all these projects we are indebted to the expertise and sheer hard graft of our Outside Works team and permanent way volunteers.

Outside Works is just one of the departments which must all work together to ensure the Museum's ongoing development and continuing operation. The average visitor probably has little idea of how many people are working behind the scenes to preserve the trams and other artefacts for the Nation, as well as to provide the public with an enjoyable and informative day out. In addition, there are official rules and guidelines regarding the care of our collections which must be followed.

National Tramway Museum

Official monitoring of museums has taken the form of increasingly stringent quality control by a succession of bodies. In particular the standing of the Museum was, for many years, reflected by its status as a Registered museum; from 2006 this has been replaced by a more comprehensive process of Accreditation, initially supervised by the Museums, Libraries and Archives Council, now Arts Council England, in which more activities, policies and procedures have to reach the required standards. It took some time for the MLA to work out how its Accreditation scheme should be applied to Independent Museums, but this was followed by the Museum gaining full Accreditation in 2010. This was renewed in 2014.

The Museum has come a long way since the decision was made to recruit our first paid employee. A great deal of planning and labour, both physical and mental, goes into organising and running a successful tourist attraction, as well as conserving and maintaining a fleet of historic vehicles, and we have long passed the point where the tasks could be managed by volunteers alone. Staffing levels on the whole have gradually increased, although, like so many establishments, we have been forced at times to refrain from replacing people who have left, and there have even been redundancies, leading to a revision of responsibilities and workload for the remaining workforce.

The total of 78,129 paying visitors for the 2014 season was a 2.5% increase on the previous year, while the 25,332 re-entries represented an increase of 26.8% on the 2013 figure. However these figures have to be seen in the context of around 100,000 paying visitors in the mid-2000s. This fall in visitor numbers, and consequent loss of income, has inevitably resulted in financial problems, and the Museum has had to control expenditure particularly carefully in recent years. Nevertheless 2014 saw a record number of 23 electric trams from the collection operating, together with three works cars, a horse tram in the form of Sheffield 15, dating from as early as 1874 and two tramcars on loan from outside organisations.

Within our workforce, job titles have changed, even the names of our departments have evolved to reflect current thinking, but the work goes on...

In recent years the most obvious change in personnel has been the re-establishment of the post of General Manager, following a period of supervision of the Museum by the TMS Board of Management. This move, intended partly to ensure the co-ordination of the different functions of the Museum, had been under consideration for some time.

Defining the General Manager's role required the responsibilities of the Board to be redefined. Once this was done, the recruitment process led to the appointment in 2013 of Tony Hill, former Director of the Museum of Science & Industry in Manchester. Mr Hill set in train a number of significant proposals for ongoing changes at the Museum, then left at the end of the season to pursue his career elsewhere. He was replaced in early 2014 by Dr Mike Galer, from Derby Museums.

Despite many personnel changes in all departments, continuity over the past ten years has been provided by the constant presence of Colin Heaton as Chairman of the TMS Board of Management, of Alison Isaacs as Catering & Retail Manager, and of Jan Barratt as Learning and Participation Manager.

The continuing importance to the Museum of our numerous volunteers cannot be over-emphasised. Their work is essential in all areas, not least in the demonstration of tramcar operation to visitors. Accommodation must be provided for those volunteers who wish to stay overnight, and 2013 saw the provision of new facilities after the demolition of Field House, which had fulfilled this role for many years. The replacement building offers purpose-built overnight accommodation, and has been named Sam Harrison House, in memory of the member whose generosity enabled the TMS to purchase Field House in the first place.

Volunteers at work. **National Tramway Museum**

Pioneers of the Museum

With the passage of time, the Museum has lost more of the people who helped to found and establish it with great foresight at a time when there was much less money around than there is today. The work done by the pioneers in the 1960s laid excellent foundations for the Museum we have now. 2007 saw the passing of Roy Brook, who bequeathed to us his extensive collection, and Geoff Smith, tramcar modeller. At the beginning of 2008 we lost Henry Priestley (still our oldest member, at 97). Vice Presidents Winstan Bond and Geoff Hyde left us in quick succession in December 2008 and January 2009. Also in 2008, former Board Members Keith Pearson and Alan Ralphs, George Paxton, Cyril Smeeton, and John Gardner passed away. Vice President George Hearse, Overhead Line Engineer and Outside Works Officer Neil Daft, Trevor Shears, and longstanding Auditor Roger Mercer left us in 2014, and 2015 has seen the passing of former Board Members Roger Benton and John Shawcross, and oldest serving volunteer and member, John Rose.

Much has already been said about the work of our Engineering, Outside Works, and Traffic departments, and it is now time to introduce the work of the others - Learning, Curatorial, Marketing and Business Development, Retail and Catering, Finance, and last but not least, Events.

Learning and participation for all ages.

National Tramway Museum

It is an inherent condition of the Museum's charitable status that it should be educational. We aim to work with young people of all ages, beginning with pre-school children and progressing through to those in further education. For under-5 visitors and their parents, activity backpacks were developed during 2006-2007, working in partnership with Amber Valley SureStart and with funding from Renaissance East Midlands. 'Tramway Tots' activity sessions have also been offered. In 2009-2010 the Museum signed up as a supporter of 'Kids in Museums' and in 2011 it was longlisted for the Kids in Museums Guardian Family Friendly Award, making Crich one of the top 20 family friendly museums in the country.

The replacement of the Lecture Room with the new Learning Centre gave the Learning Department more scope to offer educational activities to both school groups and families.

These activities change throughout the year, and are themed to tie in with the seasons and with current special events. Care has been taken to develop provision for secondary pupils as well as the many visitors from primary schools. Communities, as well as schools, have been involved in projects based around the Museum. In 2011 the Museum was awarded learning flagship status for the 'Talking Museum' project involving Crich Junior School, local residents, volunteers and staff. We were also part of the 3-year, Heritage Lottery-funded Groundwork Nottingham Tram Travellers project, in which pupils from 11 schools, having visited the Museum, worked with their local communities and Nottingham Express Transit to compare first and second generation tramways.

School Visit.
National Tramway Museum

Colleges and Universities benefit from our educational facilities and expertise too. The Museum has been involved in everything from taster days and work placements to collaboration in projects such as Leicester University's 2012-2013 research into the impact of museums on health and wellbeing.

Learning is not only for children, however. The Learning Department's aim is to encourage all visitors, whatever their age, abilities or background, to acquire a piece of knowledge during their visit, or take a new skill away with them. The Department has been involved in researching and producing content for the various exhibitions, to ensure that these will engage and inform the widest possible range of visitors; and during the school holidays of 2007, Family Learning was introduced, giving families the opportunity to be creative together.

In 2011, the Museum was awarded the Sandford Award for Heritage Education; this is only one example of the numerous awards which have been made to the Museum for its educational work over recent years.

To enhance the visitor experience the presence of Guides has been formalised. In 2014 timed Guided Tours were introduced, which have provided a viewpoint for our visitors of the structures that form the backdrop to the tramway and the creation of an urban environment. Their popularity has ensured they are now a regular feature.

All these methods benefit the Museum, firstly by providing a more interesting and varied experience for visitors, who are therefore more likely to return, but also by strengthening the Museum's chances of attracting funding, since major funding bodies expect to see their money making a difference to visitors' lives.

The Curatorial Department is responsible for the care of the Museum's collections. This includes not only the trams themselves, but also tram-related memorabilia, together with many thousands of items seldom seen by the public – chiefly books, journals and photographs.

The John Price Memorial Library has gained much by the generous financial support of Trevor and Lyn Shears, through the Shears Foundation – sadly Trevor's passing in 2014 meant that the Museum lost another good friend. This support has helped the Library and Archive to become the most comprehensive in its field in the world.

The Archive's already outstanding collections are constantly being enhanced by more incoming written and visual material, as it acquires acknowledged major collections. Archive material relating to both traditional tramways and new generation tramways is available to researchers throughout the year. Students, genealogists, authors and book editors are among those who have utilised our archive in the past, and continue to do so. Recent donations have included the British Electric Traction Minute Books (in no fewer than 27 Archive boxes, received in 2007), Edgar Allen's drawings of track layouts, more than 200 books, models, slides and negatives from the Alan Askew estate in 2010, and the Ken Sutton collection in 2014.

In 2008, the purchase of roller racking for the Library was funded by a donation from Winstan Bond in anticipation of his collection coming to the Museum. In the same year, other major tasks included the extensive Winstan Bond collection being catalogued (then subsequently cleaned and conserved), and David Tudor digitising the 2,000 pages of Jim Halsall's collection of information on the tramways of Blackburn and Darwen.

Co-operation with the Light Rail Operators Group has seen material from the new generation of tramway operators presented to the Library, ensuring that this period of transport history has its due place in the museum archives.

Exhibiting at Group Leisure Exhibition 2012.

National Tramway Museum

The marketing of the Museum and its Special Events has developed and improved greatly over the past ten years. Promotional material such as leaflets, posters and banners, and advertising in various formats and locations, has been used to its full extent.

The promotion of the Best of Sheffield Week is a good example of how these methods can be used to bring a specific event to the attention of its target audience.

The primary purposes in organising this event were firstly, to make more Sheffield residents aware of the existence of the Museum, and secondly, to attract more visitors from that area. To make the people of Sheffield aware of the Museum, the restoration of Sheffield 510, and the Best of Sheffield Week, an item appeared on BBC Look North, interviews were given to Radio Sheffield, and articles appeared in the local press. Targeted group mailings were sent out, and leaflets were put on display in local shops, libraries, Tourist Information Centres, etc. Local transport enthusiasts assisting with leaflet

Website and Social Media site.

distribution. Visitor surveys indicate that these methods did succeed in attracting more visitors from Sheffield to the event, and to the Museum for repeat visits.

On an everyday basis, joint promotions with Amber Valley Tourism and other organisations have increased awareness, while the Museum's corporate identity has been developed through various branding strategies. Signage, stationery, promotional items, literature, vehicle livery, staff badges and logos have all been redesigned to conform to the Museum's house style and to reinforce its image.

A substantial form of promotion has been the website. The internet has expanded greatly over the last decade as a means of communication, both with prospective visitors and with members of the TMS. Electronic booking of duties for drivers and conductors has become a particularly useful facility, especially when around 150 members volunteer for operational duties each year. The Museum website was modernised in March 2010, a year which also saw the arrival of a new blog, and Facebook and Twitter pages were added to the informal social networking that was already taking place. Online ticketing was made available in 2012.

In the last couple of years we have moved away from regional TV advertising and towards targeted radio campaigns. The BBC TV drama *A Passionate Woman,* starring Billie Piper, was partly filmed at the Museum in 2009, as was the feature film *Sightseers,* released in November 2012. In 2011 the Museum helped with the production of a television documentary, *The Golden Age of Tramways,* in the BBC4 Timeshift series. It has also appeared in a number of antiques programmes, and has also featured in news reports on the opening of Nottingham's new tram routes.

Left: The Forge Gift Shop.
Right: Rita's Tearooms.
National Tramway Museum

The retail and catering activities at the Museum underwent an important change on 1st April 2007 when they were transferred to a wholly-owned subsidiary trading company, Tramway Museum Services (R&C) Ltd. This change was to allow more flexibility and freedom from charity trading restrictions, with the intention of developing new sources of income.

The refreshment pavilion had become an ice cream facility in 2004, removing ice cream sales from the gift shop which had become a sweet shop in 2003. In 2013 improved access to the ice cream kiosk was provided.

An unexpected and very useful development has been a change in the licensing laws, making it possible to obtain a drinks licence covering all the Museum premises, not just the Red Lion building. A volunteer team successfully operates The Major's Bar at many special events resulting in the Museum becoming well known for the provision of real ale.

Both Rita's Tea Rooms and the Poulson Room Restaurant offer hot and cold food and drinks to the public, and when the new National Food Hygiene rating scheme was established, the Retail & Catering Department was delighted to achieve the maximum rating of 5 stars across all outlets.

The gift shop, formerly known as Scothern and Williamson, was re-roofed in 2011 and given a full refit in early 2015, when it was renamed The Forge (in fact a return to an earlier name for the bookshop). The sale of local craft items has developed and they continue to sell well. Catering was not neglected and Rita's Tea Rooms was refurbished and given new furniture for the 2014 season.

Finance is a department whose work is frequently forgotten by the public; and if it is remembered, it is usually not understood. Nevertheless it is the Museum's finances which enable all this work to go on, and it is the Finance Department which manages the available funds. Each Event, each project, is allocated a sum from the annual budget, and much ingenuity is often required to ensure that the best possible visitor experience results from the spending of that sum. Each department, too, has its annual budget, and it is the task of department heads to ensure that their work is carried out correctly and to the best possible standard, yet within their means.

Sponsorship and grants

As well as income from entrance fees and other visitor spending, the Museum has been able to attract funding in various ways. In speaking of the repair and renovation of our trams, we have already acknowledged the importance of funding from bodies such as the Tramcar Sponsorship Organisation, the Transport Trust, the Scottish Tramway & Transport Society, the Fylde Society, the London County Council Tramways Trust, Dorlec and Scotts. In addition the Museum has successfully applied for grants and awards from organisations such as the Derbyshire Economic Partnership and the Wolfson Foundation (for the redesign of the Exhibition Hall, as described earlier), the Heritage Lottery Fund (for the reconstruction of the former Stone Workshop), and others. Society members have often made generous donations towards work on trams and other projects.

Completing applications for grants can be an extremely time-consuming and complex task, and the wait to learn if the application has been successful or not can be lengthy, but without such supplements to the Museum's funds, much of our development work could not continue.

One area in which the work of all Departments (except perhaps that of Finance, which as ever operates largely behind the scenes, but nevertheless underpins everything) will be evident to the observant visitor is that of our Special Events. Here, more than anywhere else, all the disciplines must work together to ensure that the day – or weekend, or week – is a success.

These Special Events continue to be an important part of the Museum's appeal, their attendance figures reflecting their popularity with the public. They also inspire considerable efforts on the part of Museum volunteers and people visiting the Museum as part of the show, whether as re-enactors or as drivers of vintage vehicles.

Some events focus on the trams, such as the host of vehicles turned out for Tramathons and Enthusiasts' Days, while others are more general. The general events offer a wide variety of very popular experiences based on the Museum and its collections, ranging from Emergency Vehicles Day and the 1940s events to Starlight Halloween and Beside the Seaside - possibly the most unlikely occurrence so far away from the sea, and nearly 1,000 feet up in the Derbyshire hills.

In the past, events took place only at weekends, but in 2014 the Best of Sheffield, Beside the Seaside and Starlight Halloween events were all extended to see if a longer period of operation would bring in more visitors. This has continued through into 2015.

Public tastes are always changing, and our Special Events programme needs to evolve if it is to continue to attract visitors, both new and repeat.

For over sixty years our Events have been organised and run almost entirely by volunteers. This must be regarded as a singular achievement.

Let us look in more detail at some of our recent landmark events.

The annual Enthusiasts' Day was extended to a weekend in 2012 when it was combined with an event commemorating the 50th anniversary of the closure of the Glasgow tramway system. The *Glasgow 50* part of the event featured five Glasgow trams – 22, 812, 1068, 1115 and 1282. 1115 was put on display outside for the first time in several years, having featured in displays in both the old and new Exhibition Halls. When all five trams were lined up on the Depot Fan, visitors could enjoy and appreciate the rare sight of all five Glasgow route colours together. The four operational trams were run in procession and also carried passengers, as well as providing plenty of photo opportunities for enthusiasts.

Glasgow tramcars at the Glasgow 50 event displaying four different upper deck coloured bands as used for visually identifying separate routes.

Malcolm Wright

This was the day Glasgow 1068, previously seen at Crich as Paisley 68 (its original format), was unveiled in its new livery. It also returned to short-term operation for the first time since 2009, when it had been withdrawn because of wheel problems.

The tram had entered the Workshop earlier in the year. In a transformation sponsored by the Scottish Tramway & Transport Society, it was given, as well as new paintwork in orange and cream, a new blue route colour on the top deck decency panels, to display a further feature unique among the Glasgow trams at Crich. It is the only open-topped Glasgow tram to be preserved, apart from the horse tram in Glasgow.

During its stay in the Workshop it was established that 1068's bodywork was in better condition than expected, and it was hoped that, with a certain amount of work on this, it would eventually be able to return to operation.

Another highlight of the event occurred when the workshop became the stage for a recreation of Glasgow's Coplawhill works, with all five trams in residence.

An event showcasing the Brush Company's contribution to tramcar building and development was also organised in 2012, to coincide with and celebrate the launch of Blackpool 630. Chesterfield 7, Leeds 180 and LPTB 1622 were in service, while other Brush tramcars were brought out to provide displays and photo opportunities, and two Brush-bodied buses were in attendance. 630 emerged from the depot ready for its launch ceremony, afterwards being presented alongside Blackpool trams 2 and 762; the tramcar then set off on its first passenger-carrying journey since leaving Blackpool. Passengers who had paid for a seat on 630's first run next enjoyed a guided tour of the Workshop.

Later in the day Douglas Southern Electric Tramways 1 was brought out of the Exhibition Hall and displayed on the depot fan; this tramcar was built in 1896 at the Falcon Works, Loughborough, which was later taken over by the Brush Company.

The day ended with two competition winners being given the chance to drive 630.

A remarkable event, *London came to Crich*, on 5th October 2013, took the form of a UK Railtours charity excursion from London St Pancras by East Midlands Trains HST. This raised the marvellous sum of £95,400 for the Railway Children charity, which supports children who live on the streets in Britain and overseas.

Variety at Crich is provided by horse tram operation, with 1874 veteran Sheffield 15 running along the street. This has typically occurred during the Edwardian weekend, but it was such a successful feature of the *Best of Sheffield* event in 2014 that horse tram operation was extended to become a regular mid-week experience for visitors in 2015.

The idea of creating an event for enthusiasts based around the relaunch of Sheffield 510 originated with Crich's tram crews. The concept was taken up by the Marketing and Business Development Department who were aware that fewer people from Sheffield were coming to Crich than might have been expected, given the city's proximity to the Museum, and given also that the Sheffield tram system had closed only in 1960, well within living memory for many. As explained earlier, it was hoped that organising and promoting the event would make more Sheffield residents want to visit the Museum. An opportunity was also taken to stage a week-long event instead of the usual day or weekend.

Passengers on the UK Railtours excursion alight for transport to Crich 2013.
National Tramway Museum

510's overhaul and repaint has already been described. It is interesting to note that the 'Last Tram' livery, only originally intended to last for a week, had been in place for 50 years, so it was long overdue for restoration work.

Horse car Sheffield 15 now provides some mid-week experiences.

John Burton

After its launch ceremony, 510 made an inaugural run with members of the TSO and other invited guests on board; after this it entered regular operation.

Crich's other operational Sheffield tram, 74, also ran in service, while 189 and works car 330 posed for photographs on the depot fan. Some visiting Sheffield buses, plus other vintage vehicles with connections to Sheffield, were also on display. In addition, the Red Lion served real ales brewed in the city. Towards the end of the first day of the event a mini-cavalcade was formed from Sheffield trams 15, 74, 510 and 330.

With the Sunday presented as a family-oriented event rather than a day for enthusiasts, and each weekday themed and designed to appeal to visiting groups, the visitor numbers and spending figures throughout the Museum were sufficient to increase the possibility of other week-long events in the future.

Electric 50

The 50th anniversary of electric tramcar operation at Crich, celebrated in 2014, was an occasion which called for an extremely special celebration. Preparations for it began two years in advance, when Blackpool & Fleetwood 2 and Southampton 45 were withdrawn from service pending future overhauls. Withdrawing them early meant that there would be sufficient operating life in them to reactivate them for the 2014 season, enabling them to take part in the Electric 50 celebrations.

It was decided that a cavalcade of 25 trams should be presented on each of the two days. Most of these could be supplied from the Museum's running fleet, but sourcing the remainder was not so simple.

Blackpool & Fleetwood 'Box' 40 was in Blackpool on a long-term loan. It was agreed that the tram should be overhauled (a joint project with Blackpool Transport) and brought back to Crich for the occasion. Also from Blackpool came Balloon 711, while Newcastle 114 was loaned from Beamish Museum. Blackpool 167 went to

Far right: Electric 50 cavalcade.

National Tramway Museum

ELECTRIC 50

50 YEARS OF ELECTRIC TRAMS AT CRICH

Electric 50 Traffic Staff 2014.
Malcolm Wright

both Beamish and Blackpool in exchange, but was brought back to Crich in time for the *Electric 50* weekend.

Testing Newcastle 114 and re-commissioning the returned Blackpool 167 kept the Museum's engineers extremely busy in the run-up to the event. In addition there was work to be done on other trams. MET 331 was repaired in time after having been damaged during a derailment, but sadly LCC 106 could not be made ready, as it was still receiving attention in the Workshop as part of its latest overhaul.

On the day before the event, the three visiting trams were all running, providing a unique experience for visitors, while Museum staff and volunteers were hard at work behind the scenes, dealing with the myriad tasks which must always be completed if a major event is to be a success. Operating 25 trams of course meant that 25 tram crews had to be found, organised, and catered for. The helpful signs and leaflets our visitors expect had to be prepared, and the public address system set up so Museum staff could explain to them what they were seeing. At the same time, trams were being shunted into the correct positions, ready for the morrow.

Each cavalcade, although featuring the same trams, was to be different: in the first, the vehicles would be presented in the order they had first operated at the Museum; in the second, the history and development of the tramcar would be illustrated. In addition, displays and photo opportunities, featuring groups of 'related' trams, were set up. To ensure that as many people as possible had a chance to ride on all the trams, the Traffic Department did all they could to keep 15 vehicles operational at all times on both days. This resulted in more organising, as trams had to be sent back to the depot in the correct order, ready to be assembled into the afternoon's cavalcade. Mike Crabtree was

Part of the Electric 50 cavalcade.
National Tramway Museum

praised by all, but particularly by event leaders James Blythe and Dan Heeley, for his work in planning tram movements, which made the whole spectacle possible.

There were also a few surprises for visitors. So many tram crews were available on the Sunday that it was possible to add Sheffield 330 and Cardiff 131 to the cavalcade, making 27 tramcars in all. Glasgow 1068 made an appearance, replacing 812 which had suffered mechanical failure. And last but not least, Southampton 45 joined the cavalcade on its last day in service before being withdrawn for overhaul.

The whole event was a prime example of what can be achieved when staff and volunteers from all departments work together to make a major event a success.

In September 2005 HRH Duke of Gloucester visited the Museum and unveiled a plaque to mark the restoration and installation of the Reading Corporation men's urinal; while on 20th August 2009 the standing of the Museum and the significance of its collections were marked by the unveiling of a Transport Trust Red Wheel plaque on the wall of the Exhibition Hall by Transport Trust President Sir William McAlpine.

The Museum lies in the Parliamentary constituency of Derbyshire Dales, whose MP, the Rt Hon. Patrick McLoughlin, was appointed Secretary of State for Transport in September 2012. Mr McLoughlin visited the Museum the following month, and gained the hands-on experience available at Crich (and also enjoyed by many participants in the Ultimate Tram Driving Experience) by driving Southampton 45 during his visit.

In July 2013 HRH Duke of Gloucester returned to help us celebrate the 50th anniversary of horse tram service, and was pleased to take the opportunity to drive Sheffield 15 and Blackpool 'Boat' 236.

Meanwhile a licence to hold civil weddings was granted in 2013, and the first of these took place at the Museum on 29th June of that year.

The extensive buildings at the Museum represent an exceptional asset. Particular mention must be made of the Depot complex, which is a continuing tribute to the members who had the wisdom to get the trams under cover as fast as possible in the 1960s. It has served the Museum well, though naturally a few shortcomings have become apparent over the years. In the medium term it is hoped to fit it with new doors and improved insulation to give the trams an environment less affected by the climatic conditions which can occur high up in the Derbyshire hills, especially in the winter. In the longer term there are plans for new interpretative displays within the Depot complex together with a new exhibition area to house 35-50 trams. This project would enable more extensive workshop and general conservation facilities to be provided, as well as giving more room to display the unique collections of tramcars and other exhibits.

A number of other schemes that would enhance the Museum have been identified. The Museum has been left funding towards the construction of a replica Manchester Corporation bogie tramcar, while another rolling stock project is the restoration of a second Beyer Peacock steam tram (held in store in dismantled condition) to haul the Dundee trailer.

A completely new entrance building will eventually be required. Modern conference facilities are envisaged, while other possible buildings are a cinema, a fish and chip shop, and some reconstructed Edwardian houses and shops to add substance to the concept of Crich Tramway Village.

Top: The Patron HRH Duke of Gloucester takes the controller key for Blackpool 236 from Martin Gurr, July 2013

Centre: Secretary of State for Transport ,Rt. Hon Patrick McLoughlin takes control of Southampton 45, October 2012

Bottom: Transport Trust President Sir William McAlpine unveils the Red Wheel plaque with President Cheryl Cunningham and Chairman Colin Heaton

National Tramway Museum

The Tramway Museum Society - an operating record of tramcars at the Museum

CAR	SYSTEM	MILEAGE TO DEC 2014	WORKSHOP ATTENTION	OPERATED AT NTM (IN YEARS)
PASSENGER CARS:				
1	Derby	display	paint	display, never ran
1	Douglas Southern	display	minor	occasionally
1	London County C		14	never
2	Blackpool & F'wood	22,629	77, 85, 98, 10	66-8, 70-6, 78-83, 86-02, 05-12, 14
4	Blackpool	display	minor	occasionally
5	Gateshead	13,744	76, 88-9, 00	68-70, 77-82, 87, 89-92, 96-99, 01-07
5	Blackpool		no	in store, never ran
7	Chesterfield	15,188	95-7, 06	97 on
8	Chesterfield (a)		no	occasionally
9	Oporto		paint	occasionally
10	Howth (b)		no	display
14	Grimsby and Imm'm	display	paint	never
15	Sheffield	n/a	93/4	63-64 and one weekend a year. 14-3 days, 15-3 days
21	Dundee	display	minor	display
22	Glasgow (c)	40,023	70, 75, 86,94, 97, 02, 15	66-9, 71-9, 81-3, 87-01, 03-14,
35	Edinburgh (d)	8	13 - conservation work	89, then display
40	Blackpool (e)	40,644	71, 82-3, 97, 99, 07	64-5, 74-8, 84 on
40	Blackpool & F'wood (f)	521	64-5, 14	14
45	Southampton	26,972	77, 84-7, 95, 07	64-6, 77-82, 88-94, 96-12, 14
46	Sheffield	542	minor	64-8, 70-3
49	Blackpool	17,381	76	64-73, 75, 77-92
52	Gateshead		no	in store, never ran. Transferred to Beamish 2014
59	Blackpool (g)	890	minor	65, 67-90; in store
60	Johannesburg	19,677	76/7, 84, 97	77-83, 85-93, 97-99, 02, 06-12
68 (1068)	Paisley (Glasgow) (h)	27,326	77, 87, 94, 02, 12	78-93, 95-97, 99-09, 12 on
74	Sheffield	13,398	93 5, 99, 05	95 on
76	Leicester	658	minor	73 5
102	Newcastle (i)	6,561	78/9, 88, 94,	75-7, 80-1, 89-90, 92-4, 99-00
106	London County C'l	20,225	82/3, 94, 97, 00, 13/14	83-92, 95-99, 02-07, 10, 15
132	Hull	display	no	on loan

CAR	SYSTEM	MILEAGE TO DEC 2014	WORKSHOP ATTENTION	OPERATED AT NTM (IN YEARS)

PASSENGER CARS:

CAR	SYSTEM	MILEAGE TO DEC 2014	WORKSHOP ATTENTION	OPERATED AT NTM (IN YEARS)
159	London United	1,080	05-12	12 on
166	Blackpool	13,848	73/4, 03, 10	74-92, 95/96, 04-06, 08, 09, 11 on
167	Blackpool (j)	23,735	85, 98, 00, 09	85-98, 01-08, 10 on
180	Leeds	27,984	81, 91, 97, 08	68-73, 82-08, 10 on
180	Prague	13,040	minor	68-71, 73-97, 01
189	Sheffield	1,586	minor	66-72, 74-6, 78-80
236	Blackpool	3,898	no	12 on
249	Blackpool	display	no	display
264	Sheffield	3,152	minor	70-80
273	Oporto	3,699	98-00,13	95, 01-06, 08-10,14 on
298	Blackpool		no	not run
331	Metropolitan Elec. (k)	14,451	88, 92-3, 08	88-91, 94-98, 00 on
345	Leeds	6,077	03-05, 10	05-09, 12 on
399	Leeds	22,629	88/9, 00,10	90-99, 01-07, 09 on
510	Sheffield	24,387	80/1, 92, 98, 03,12	64-72, 76-9, 82-91, 93-97, 99-01, 03-06, 14 on
600	Leeds	221	no	69, 71, 72
602	Leeds	5,531	73, 77, 86, 04	67, 72, 75-6, 79-80, 87-95, 03-06
630	Blackpool	1,392	11	12 on
674	New York 3rd Ave	6,415	no	70-5, 77-85
762	Blackpool	43	11-13	14 on
765	Manchester (l)	1,133	minor	77-8
812	Glasgow	28,550	78/9, 84, 91	66-77, 80-90, 92-7, 99-02, 04 on, 98, 03
869	Liverpool	12,224	91-3, 99, 14	93-99, 00-11, 15
902	Halle	277	05	05 06
1100	Glasgow	2,068	no	65-76
1115	Glasgow	1,976	no	71-76
1147	The Hague	display	paint	display, never ran
1282	Glasgow	14,926	77-8, 86, 96	78-85, 86-7, 90-5, 97-03,12
1297	Glasgow (m)	5,330	79, 87 , 05	69-78, 80-6, 88-9, 06-7
1622	London Transport	9,376	94-96, 99,07	97-8, 00-06, 08 on
223-006	Berlin	14,441	96-7, 11	96 on

The Tramway Museum Society - an operating record of tramcars at the Museum

CAR	SYSTEM	MILEAGE TO DEC 2014	WORKSHOP ATTENTION	OPERATED AT NTM (IN YEARS)

WORK CARS ETC:

CAR	SYSTEM	MILEAGE TO DEC 2014	WORKSHOP ATTENTION	OPERATED AT NTM (IN YEARS)
I	Glasgow Mains Dept		no	never ran
2	Blackpool		no	in 70s, now in store
TW2	Leeds		minor	69-09
W21	Glasgow		no	never ran, in store
47	Steam loco (n)		no	last steamed in 85; display
65	Oporto coal transporter		no	in store
96	Brussels snowbroom		minor	display
717	Blackpool	85		66 on
-	Eades reversible truck		no	display
131	Cardiff (o)	07-8		09 on
330	Sheffield		minor	every year
KLV	Croydon Tramlink		minor	10 on

MOTOR WORKS VEHICLES:

UB7931	Leeds	Dennis recovery vehicle
CWJ510	Sheffield	AEC Tower Wagon

HORSE DRAWN WORKS VEHICLES:

	Manchester	Tower Wagon

Notes:

(a)   On loan from Science Museum, but at NTM;
(b)   Ran in Blackpool, no mileage data;
(c)   Includes 3,852 miles at Glasgow Garden Festival;
(d)   Also ran 3,883 miles at Glasgow GF, and at Blackpool 1985-8;
(e)   Also 1,760 miles at Blackpool 1985;
(f)   Loaned out, ran at Blackpool and Heaton Park;
(g)   Ran at Blackpool 1980-90
(h)   1068 operated at Beamish in 2013;
(i)   Also ran 1,257 miles at Gateshead GF;
(j)   Also 2,345 miles at Blackpool 1985, 1,922 miles at Gateshead GF. Also ran 3,802 miles at Blackpool and 4,109 miles at Glasgow GF; Blackpool and Beamish in 2014;
(k)   Also 2127 miles at GF as Sunderland 100;
(l)   Has also run at Heaton Park and Blackpool;
(m)   Also ran 3,802 miles at Blackpool and 4,109 miles at Glasgow GF;
(n)   Also ran at Blackpool, 1985;
(o)   131 operated in Blackpool in 2012; .

In these tables the term 'workshop attention' includes overhauls, restoration and repainting, but excludes routine maintenance. Compiled from information kindly supplied by Malcolm Wright.

The TMS owns a number of other tramcar bodies, trucks and other components which are in store. Mention must be made of the three locomotives which the Museum has owned over the years, 'Rupert', 'Ted' and 'GMJ' which have all played their part in the construction and maintenance of the Museum tramway.